Creative Content for the Web

To Kim

Acknowledgements

I would like to thank Paul Honeywill, my MA tutor in Publishing at the University of Plymouth, for encouraging me to write this book. Colin Searls, Visual Arts Subject Leader at the University of Plymouth, has been a source of lively and always thought provoking debate about new media content and the directions and developments of web technologies and their subsequent impact on content. I've also enjoyed greatly discussing the impact of the web and its potential to create new opportunities, perhaps even new forms of content in the creative arts with my friend Dr. David Lynn, editor of *The Kenyon Review*. At Intellect Books, Robin Beecroft has provided sensitive editorial guidance.

The phenomenon of the World Wide Web may be a recent one, but already there have been scores of books, articles, and essays written about it, proof certainly that electronic new media publishing will not bring about the death of the printed word (as some Jeremiahs would have us believe). My views and opinions have been formed and shaped by many of the influential writers and thinkers listed under Further Reading and I acknowledge my debt to them.

Last but by no means least, I would like to thank my wife Kim for all her support in my recent studies and with the creation, design and production of this book. Throughout this period, she has been a constant source of encouragement, guidance, and gentle but always unerringly wise criticism. She has been involved in too many ways to adequately enumerate, morally, spirtually, and practically.

Trademarks

Introduction

For most of the past year or so that I've been working on this book, a multinational telecommunications company has been causing havoc in the small, historic riverside hamlet where we live. Quite understandably, there has been considerable, sometimes vociferous, local grumbling and protest but I, for one, have more than welcomed its presence. Why? Because in laying fibre optic cable to every home in our small Devon town, I consider that the relatively minor inconvenience and temporary upheaval is well worth the benefits that such an important infrastructure can potentially bring: for this is one means that will facilitate the promise of the World Wide Web moving from the office into the mainstream living room; the improvement of existing narrow bandwidth that currently clogs the system and keeps it from working efficiently; the realisation of true multimedia capabilities and of interactive digital TV linked to the web; and much more. A revolution in content, publishing and communications is certainly upon us and I look forward in anticipation.

Yet, it has all happened so very quickly. For those of us who have already embraced the World Wide Web wholeheartedly, can we even remember what life was like without it? At times it seems there is talk of little else. Web sites are proliferating at an exponential rate on virtually any topic under the sun. In such a brief period of time, this utterly new phenomenon has entered into our consciousness and daily lives to such an all pervasive extent that it is no longer possible to ignore it, even should we so desire. And anyway, why should we? The World Wide Web, which only made its embryonic global appearance as recently as 1993, has emerged as the most exciting and dynamic new publishing medium around, and arguably the most significant advance in the communication of man's thought and ideas since Gutenberg's perfection of moveable type in the fifteenth century.

From a mere 130 web sites in 1993, web sites now number in the millions. Home pages for individuals are being created at an estimated rate of 10,000 per day and some predict that by the millennium, there will be some 50 million Home pages on the web. Individuals, publishers, broadcasters, corporate businesses, organisations, and institutions are all rushing headlong to create their web sites, if they have not already done so.

The aim of this book is to slow down for a moment (if that is possible in this frenzied field), to take a considered and thoughtful look at content on the web from both a theoretical and practical point of view in order to gain an understanding of the power of this new medium, as well as to consider how content on the web – creative, imaginative, above all effective content – can be produced that takes full advantage of its features and undoubted powerful capabilities. For, just as Gutenberg's perfection of moveable type led directly to the creation of new forms of published content, so does the rise of electronic publishing over the World Wide Web mark a similar watershed in the history of communicating thought and ideas, and indeed in our own relation to the world and beyond as it alters our perceptions of space, national frontiers, even reality itself, some claim.

Make no mistake, web publishing truly is like nothing that has preceded it. At once a publishing medium, a forum for live creative broadcasts (or narrowcasts), an interactive medium for direct synchronous and asynchronous communication, it empowers individuals, organisations, communities, and all who use and publish on it. But such power needs to be understood to be exploited effectively.

How the web is unique

As both a publishing and communications medium, the World Wide Web is unique in many ways. It is truly global, providing a means of sharing and retrieving information from anywhere in the world. Admittedly, the web at its inception was (and still is) predominantly US-centric, and its use certainly remains more prevalent in industrialised and developed countries even now. But it is interesting to note that the fastest areas of growth at the time of writing are developing nations. It is certain that as this trend accelerates, we'll see a similar exponential growth in native-language and localised and specialist content to cater for small, emerging, specialist and niche markets.

The fact that the Internet by design is decentralised means furthermore that content can be published outside the control of governments. By being independent of its own infrastructure, accessible over existing telephone networks anywhere in the world (and soon by wireless telecommunications technology), the system is less open to control by governments, thus making it a powerful instrument for freedom of speech throughout the world. But true freedom of speech also raises questions about censorship, and the need to have some way of dealing with irresponsible, offensive, and dangerous material.

The low cost for web usage means that barriers to access of content are minimised. Not only is the cost of creating and disseminating information low (especially compared to print), moreover, the cost of accessing content is similarly low. The decentralised structure of the Internet based on a network of networks means that the capacity to hold information is virtually unlimited, though the existing narrow bandwidth that is currently the backbone of the Internet does mean that the whole system may at times function painfully slowly. This is likely to improve as fibre optic cables, satellites, and other means of transmitting supercede telephone lines in months and years to come.

The creation of such a medium that truly enables anyone anywhere in the world to be a publisher must represent a true and momentous revolution in the communication of ideas and thoughts.

Publishing on the World Wide Web

The most cursory glance at the broadest category index of a popular search engine such as Yahoo![1] gives an indication of the comprehensive range of topics that are currently being covered on the World Wide Web: arts and humanities; business and economy; computers and the Internet; education; entertainment; government; health; news and media; recreation and sports; reference; regional; science; social science; society and culture. And this is only the tip of the iceberg, for each broad category has an enormous host of directories and sub-directories, each listing scores, sometimes hundreds or even thousands of web sites, covering topics such as news, entertainment guides, travel advice, academic research, shopping and electronic commerce, reviews of books, movies, plays and restaurants, stock prices and tips, corporate reports, and much more. Web sites exist on virtually any topic under the sun; and if no web site yet exists on some given topic, then you can bet that one will soon be created, if it hasn't already been by the time you read this.

Part of this enormous explosion in new media publishing can be explained by the simple fact that it is so relatively easy and inexpensive to publish electronically on the World Wide Web. Unlike traditional publishing, production costs can be minimal and more importantly, the costs of distributing digital information globally on-line can be considerably less than the distribution of hard copy books, magazines or newspapers. And because virtually anyone can do it, it should perhaps not be surprising that virtually everyone (or so it almost seems) *is* doing it, from massive multinational corporations spending literally hundreds of thousands of pounds on web development (and web marketing strategy), to individuals beavering away to produce their own unique Home page on a shoestring. The web, moreover, has proved itself to be a remarkably democratic publishing medium where all are equal, or almost so. Indeed, due to the continuing limitations of narrow bandwidth (which results in the slow speed of web access), spending huge sums to create a site packed with the latest all-singing, all-dancing features and buzzwords can often be counterproductive, a literal invitation to turn off or click somewhere else, while the low-budget, even no-budget site constructed intelligently by someone who is passionately interested in and dedicated to his or her chosen niche or subject can attract a global audience far greater than any reasonable expectation.

As important as the number of web sites and domains is the growing user base that has access to them. Similar exponential growth is predicted. A conservative estimate of users who currently have access to the World Wide Web is probably over 70 million. The World Trade Organisation predicts the number of Internet users will rise to more than 300 million by the turn of the century.[2] In the USA alone, over a quarter of households are currently hooked up to the Internet. Some media analysts predict that figure will jump to over 40 per cent by the year 2001, and it is not difficult to see how: web TV, interactive digital TV, and fibre optic cable promise to bring the interactivity of the web into the living room, at a stroke increasing the potential audience considerably. Indeed, it is perhaps most surprising how such an already high degree of penetration has been reached considering that access at the moment still remains almost exclusively through PCs, and thus principally linked to offices in companies, organisations, academic institutions, and homes. As access to the web moves from the office to the living room, and who knows, perhaps to the kitchen, the bathroom, the car, or your wrist, the implications and opportunities for creative content are considerable.

Indeed, it is certain that we'll see an ever more sophisticated evolution of the user interface by which we access the web (currently through web browsers that have grown ever more powerful and packed with top-heavy, memory-hungry features, but which may also at the same time have to slim down in order to be accessible on hand-held devices not yet in use or even invented). The so-called 'browsers wars', the battle for the living room as the web moves into our mainstream living spaces and the impact that such a move will have on audience and content, global convergence as a new supranational net culture defines itself through language and new media, the emergence of a new techno-underclass, those denied access or unwilling to enter into the brave new world of cyberspace: such issues need to be explored in order to gain an understanding about how the message and the medium are intertwined, and about how creative and effective content can be crafted on the web.

Creative content

The craft of producing creative web content, I stress, does not to me lie in producing web sites that sing and dance and make use of this month's latest 'killer application' or graphic pyrotechnics. Indeed, as web sites have evolved from static first generation information spaces to more complicated screen layouts using frames and tables, the games arcade phenomenon of sites that flash and move, the use of ghastly colours and moronic graphics, slow loading java applets that may be clever but add little if anything to content, have increased at a similar rate. The emergence of any new medium, naturally, involves a certain period of transition as practitioners from old media bring former working practices, which may or may not be relevant to the new form, with them. Because the medium is new and different, there are no set rules, and for a time, anything literally goes as publishers, designers, new media practitioners, and self-appointed design gurus grope to find a visual and verbal language that is effective.

Make no mistake, design on the web does matter, and there is an emerging opus of good design on the web. However, it is my belief that creative content on the web is not design-led but rather is based on a thorough understanding of how the new medium works. Indeed in web publishing, as in any publishing, the medium itself is not entirely the message, and never should be. Yet precisely because web publishing is so highly dependent on electronic and digital technologies, indeed even driven by such technologies, it is easy to lose sight of the importance of content itself, to become more and more overwhelmed by the very technology that drives and delivers it.

By its very nature and origins, new media publishing on the web undoubtedly is new and different – this is what also makes it so exciting – and so it necessarily makes very different demands on content creation. Thus from a practical point of view, Part Two of this book explores hypertext and hyperstructure; writing hypertext effectively for the web; design and style; the concept of creating virtual communities.

Finally, this book considers some of the broader issues that relate to content creation on the World Wide Web. New media publishing on the web can indeed be liberating and empowering for the individual, as it has never been easier or cheaper to publish and reach a potential world audience. Yet amidst all the euphoria, there is a real danger that electronic publishing threatens to swamp mankind under a massive regurgitation of poorly organised, written, and thought-out material, resulting for the reader in an information overload that could be terminal. The final chapter of this book looks at electronic publishing on the web within a broader social context and furthermore examines such wider issues as ethics, freedom of expression, censorship, intellectual property rights and copyright.

Plus ça change

What is almost certain is that by the time this book is published, and certainly by the time you read it, a new generation of killer applications not yet heard of or even dreamt of will have emerged; HTML, currently in its latest manifestation as HTML 4.0, will be in a newer version approved by the all powerful, all seeing W3 Consortium[3] or more probably superceded by the more powerful and flexible XML (Extensible Markup Language).[4] Who knows, perhaps even the vexing problem of the limitations of existing bandwidth (the 'pipeline' down which digital information flows and returns which, when congested, has led some wags to dub the World Wide Web the 'world wide wait') will have been solved or at least improved by delivery over fibre optic cable, satellites, or even across electricity lines.

New consumer appliances, gadgets and gizmos, meanwhile, will be literally in hand and change the way we'll access the web. Indeed, web TV is already upon us, promising (or threatening) at a stroke to move the web from the office and home office into the living room. This is but a short step to kitchen web browsers that will hang from the wall by your cooker,[5] connected to food and recipe web sites; or new personal appliances you'll be able to wear on your wrist or body. Some futurologists (and those with a stake in the industry) predict that soon few will venture anywhere without taking a hand-held electronic browser no bigger than a paperback that will plug in to access on-line guides to wherever you are in the world, thus replacing all those heavy guidebooks that you previously carted around (and that I previously wrote).

Naturally such new ways of accessing the web will result in new forms of content. Similarly, new tools for content creation will emerge and these will inevitably have an impact on the form and shape of web content itself. It is certain that the design and the look of web sites will evolve far beyond their rudimentary forms at present as the interface continues to be refined to suit changing market and consumer requirements. We look forward to analysing such developments in both an on-line forum for this book as well as in future print editions (we do not, for the record, fear just yet that the book in its present form is about to become obsolete).

Therefore, while acknowledging that change will be upon us quicker than our computer monitors can refresh themselves, this study claims to be no more than an attempt to freeze in solid, traditional print a moment in the history of the emergence of this amazing phenomenon, the World Wide Web. For we are living in historic times. Whilst researching and writing this book, scarcely a day has gone by without some significant story, some first, related to publishing on the web: a President's reputation and career threatened to be brought down by a story first published on the web; the British Chancellor of the Exchequer's 1998 budget broadcast for the first time live on the web; 'Nannygate' and the Louise Woodward case, fought out on the web with Judge Hiller Zobel presenting his controversial judgement on the web direct and without intermediation; reports of the first sinister cases of web stalking; the first ever successful prosecution of an ISP for the delivery of pornographic content over the web; the release of Kenneth Starr's long awaited report on the Clinton/Lewinsky affair published in full and salacious detail on the web; the world's first revolution (in Indonesia) facilitated through the use of the Internet; even the broadcast by the American Health Network of the first live delivery of a baby on the web. These and scores of other stories have dominated the news in recent months and weeks.

Certainly in years (perhaps in only weeks) to come, the examples cited in the following pages may come to seem dated, the stories themselves faded to a distant memory as new subjects and issues come to the fore. Yet as the web emerges as a mainstream publishing medium, it is important in these early days to document this brief moment in history in an attempt to understand the nature and power of that which is emerging, evolving, and taking shape before our very eyes.

For it seems entirely probable that the web in its present form, or something broadly similar, is here to stay (though it would be a brave man or woman who bet their fortune on it, so sweeping are the winds of change in our ever shifting digital landscape). And while accepting that much will inevitably change as the medium continues to evolve, it is certainly my hope that many of the principles and theories that relate to creative and effective content on the web – hypertext, structure, navigation, interactivity, good writing, basic design, the concept of community, and more – will remain valid, even long after a new generation of tools has been introduced and a new generation has grown up that accepts the web as a part of normal daily life, the source of information, entertainment, and knowledge, the repository of human thought as well as the most powerful, democratic, and globally accessible publishing medium on earth.

Marc Millon
April 1999
Topsham, Devon
http:www.quaypress.com

1 Yahoo! is a search directory that catalogues and categorises web sites, and as such is itself one of the most visited sites on the World Wide Web. In addition to the main site, http://www.yahoo.com, there are now local, regional and national sites, such as for the UK: http://www.yahoo.co.uk.

2 According to a WTO report published 20 March 1998 as reported in an article 'Internet pushes back the boundaries of trade', *The Guardian* 20 March 1998, p. 25

3 The W3 Consortium, directed by World Wide Web inventor Tim Berners-Lee, is a consortium that includes over 200 companies and institutions that has charged itself with maintaining the integrity of the web by attempting to exert control over officially approved standards relating to HTML, style sheets, XML and much else. The W3 web site is of considerable importance as a web development resource: http://www.w3.org.

4 Also developed by W3 and released in February 1998, XML is a powerful meta-language based on SGML that will enable the creation of unlimited numbers of community or application specific document types. It will not replace HTML but rather work above it on another level, adding greater degrees of interactivity, control over content display, and more powerful linking capabilities, among other features.

5 The first of such appliances, a microwave oven with an integrated web browser, is due to be released in early 1999. Such smart appliances, it is envisaged, will eventually even be able to determine your shopping requirements and order groceries direct over the World Wide Web.

PART ONE

Content and the World Wide Web

CHAPTER ONE

The Birth of a New Medium

In the beginning was the Word, and the Word was with God, and the Word was God...and the Word was made flesh and dwelt among us.

The Gospel According to St. John

From oral narrative to the invention of writing; from myths, legends, stories and histories literally etched in stone, through medieval manuscripts to the printing press; from private communication between individuals, through mass media broadcasting, to electronic telecommunications and information dissemination across networks of networks interconnected globally if not yet galactically:[1] technological advancements have progressively enabled the spread of the Word and words – the communication of human thought – ever more effectively from private to public.

At its most simplistic, what Johann Gutenberg's invention did was to allow the Word – and it is fitting that his lasting monument is the Gutenberg Bible – to be mass not hand produced, and ultimately to be distributed and sold together with other written works. Previously the written and published word in Europe remained within the provenance mainly of religious orders and scholars who kept alive intellectual thought, literature and the cornerstones of Western civilisation through the hand copying on parchment and paper of the so-called illuminated manuscripts.

It is perhaps equally fitting in our modern secular age that Tim Berners-Lee's recent but no less significant invention, the World Wide Web, was created originally for no other reason than the diffusion and distribution of scientific material shared by particle physicists at the CERN Laboratories in Switzerland and their colleagues around the world. For Gutenberg's and Berners-Lee's concerns are precisely the same: the sharing and distribution of human thought and information, in the former case physically in the form of print, in the latter, literally metaphysically, as digitised information distributed invisibly and electronically.[2]

It is interesting to consider how the creation of a new technological medium impacts on our own perceptions of the world and in the process enables new forms of content to be created. If moveable type, for example, led to the rise of secular texts written in the vernacular and eventually to the creation of the novel; or if new media such as television just a few decades ago shifted our senses away from the printed word back to a world in which information and entertainment is absorbed visually leaving little if anything to the imagination, so has the emergence of the World Wide Web not only already revolutionised our access to information and communication on a global scale, but furthermore begun to challenge our very perceptions of the world we inhabit. Just as the medieval world was never quite the same after the rise of the printed word, so is the world that we are moving into already being inexorably altered and challenged by the impact of this brave new medium, as it subtly but directly challenges our fundamental concepts of linear narrative, national frontiers, space, even self and reality.

Yet so new, so very young is this already hugely powerful phenomenon that in order to understand its potential impact, in order to understand the basis and structure of the new forms of content that it enables to be produced, indeed in order to understand what creative content on the web is all about and, perhaps more importantly, what it has the potential to become, it is necessary to consider briefly the origins of the World Wide Web.

From little acorns....

The Internet is of course much larger and older than the relatively infantile World Wide Web, which inhabits just a small (though ever growing) corner of it. Begun in the 1960s during the height of the Cold War and originally funded by the US military, its earliest manifestation was originally known as ARPANET and was developed as a non-centralised means of sharing and distributing messages and communication across computer networks based on the then radical principle of open architecture networking as a means of interconnecting different networks. Should one of those networks go down for whatever reason, the digitised information would be re-routed to its intended destination by other means and paths. This non-centralised system was designed to enable the connection and communication between computers, regardless of make, platform, or operating system. Thus, a robust and in theory virtually indestructible network of computers was established that quickly grew ever more intertwined and comprehensive; by this means military intelligence, scientific and other information was able to be exchanged electronically.

As the threat of nuclear war between the superpowers receded and the Cold War eventually ceased, the military information network that was already in place was expanded as other networks, such as the National Science Foundation Network (NSFNET) linked into it, bringing what has come to be called the Internet to academic institutions and research agencies among others.

One such research organisation is CERN, the *Centre Européen de la Recherche Nucléaire* or European Centre for Particle Physics. It was at CERN that Tim Berners-Lee developed the World Wide Web in the early 1990s (prototyped in 1990-91, fully accepted over 1993-94). In an early electronic document (WWW Summary 1992) that foreshadows what surely Berners-Lee himself could never have envisaged, he writes:

> The [WWW] project is based on the philosophy that much academic information should be freely available to anyone. It aims to allow information sharing within internationally dispersed teams, and the dissemination of information by support groups. Originally aimed at the High Energy Physics community, it has spread to other areas and attracted much interest in user support, resource discovery and collaborative work areas.[3]

Many of the essential principles and fundamental elements of the World Wide Web were outlined or foreshadowed in this early but far-sighted document, most notably the concept of hyperlinked documents that collectively have the potential to create a powerful global information system. The general concept inherent in this vision is that all information from whatever source can be accessed by anyone, in any country, using any type of computer platform. The key to what eventually came to be known as the World Wide Web lay in creating and establishing a universal Internet protocol by which means smart servers (the host computers on which such documents would be stored) and smart browsers (the software program through which a user would access such documents) could understand each other. Furthermore, not only did Berners-Lee consider it essential that documents could be accessed easily across different computer platforms, equally essential to his vision was that material could be just as easily published.

Thus, in that original document he stressed the ease of creating and accessing information through what he called 'a web': 'Making a web is as simple as writing a few SGML files which point to your existing data....The very small start-up effort is designed to allow small contributions.'[4]

Even with hindsight, looking back it is hard to imagine now how Berners-Lees' remarkably simple sounding yet wholly visionary project was able to establish itself so rapidly on a global basis, especially given the infighting and cut-throat competition by which both the computing and academic worlds are so notoriously riven. Indeed, though we now accept that the world has successfully and thoroughly been networked utilising common internationally accepted protocols, it was not always like this. Ben Segal, CERN's first TCP/IP Coordinator (Internet protocol coordinator) recalls in his 'Short History of Internet Protocols at CERN':

> In the beginning was – chaos. In the same way that the theory of high energy physics interactions was itself in a chaotic state up until the early 1970s, so was the so-called area of 'Data Communications' at CERN. The variety of different techniques, media and protocols used was staggering; open warfare existed between many manufacturers' proprietary systems, various homemade systems (including CERN's own 'FOCUS' and 'CERNET'), and the then rudimentary efforts at defining open or international standards.[5]

Common Internet protocols gradually began to become established through the 1980s, and it was CERN's leading involvement in such matters which undoubtedly gave the organisation such influence in the Internet world, especially throughout Europe. Indeed by 1990, CERN's Internet presence had become the largest in Europe, and this simple fact combined with the brilliant workability of Berners-Lee's invention influenced the acceptance of its Internet protocol both in Europe and elsewhere, thus paving the way for a truly worldwide network of networks.

A new global publishing medium

In just a handful of years Berners-Lee's seemingly simple, almost modest sounding invention has created what has already proved to be an entirely new global publishing medium. Based on a protocol known as HTTP (Hypertext Transfer Protocol), web sites are accessed through their own unique URL (Universal Resource Locator), a network-wide system of addressing that describes any object anywhere on the Internet, and usually comes in a form something like http://www.mywebsite.com. The pages of the document themselves are created using a markup language known as HTML (Hypertext Markup Language) that is itself a simplified system based on existing SGML (Standard Generalised Markup Language), the international standard for defining the structure and content of electronic documents.

In the case of HTML, tags or instructions are embedded in the document to format it and these can be understood by 'smart servers' and 'smart browsers', regardless of computer platform. Such tags not only help to define the appearance of a document (for example, words that are meant to be viewed in bold type can be distinguished by tags such as <B> for bold or <EM> for emphasis), they also are used to create the hyperlinks which allow documents to interlink and cross-reference either within themselves or with other documents located on the same or even remote servers anywhere in the world.

Equally inherent within Berners-Lee's original vision of the World Wide Web was the belief that this ought to be a system that is structure- and content-oriented, not appearance-oriented. Aware that computer users throughout the world (and even just within the original limited audience of particle physicists) would be using different computer platforms, operating systems, and browsers to access a web, he devised a system that was entirely platform independent and which did not define precisely how a document should be displayed at the users' end. Indeed, Berners-Lee's original HTML was an exceedingly simple markup language that aimed to describe the logical structure of the document instead of its visual formatting and layout. Basically, the intention was to allow a document to be displayed effectively no matter what platform or browser a user had, from, at the most basic level, the display of plain text only, to more elaborate displays with some degree of text formatting and layout.

It is important, in the light of how the web has subsequently evolved, to understand that inherent in Berners-Lee's original concept was the overriding principle that it is the user ultimately who should decide how a document is displayed, not the content creator. Thus, for example, the user may through his/her browser preferences decide the size and colour of the type, default typeface, whether hyperlinks are displayed as underlined or not, whether images are displayed or not displayed at all, and many other such variables that determine how a document appears on the user's own computer screen. This essential point emphasises that the World Wide Web, from its outset, was designed to be structure-oriented not appearance-oriented, and so it remains to a large measure today: users on almost any computer platform, even the most rudimentary, should be and are still able to access content on the web, regardless of whether they can receive that content in the appearance, design, form or format that its creator intended. This essential underlying philosophy is therefore still crucial for content creators to bear in mind even now, though subsequent developments, the on-going evolution of HTML, and the potential powers enabled by XML have gone and will continue to go a long way towards granting greater and greater control to the content creator and designer.

As early as 1993, the Mosaic browser, which first allowed the integration of images with text among other innovations, led to the development of extensions to HTML which gave the medium new capabilities, the start of a general trend that continues today. As proprietory browser vendors seek to extend these capabilities ever further, notably Netscape, Microsoft and others, different subsets of HTML extensions were created which would only work on one browser platform or another. In part to standardise HTML and to safeguard the operability, accessibility and on-going evolution of the World Wide Web, the World Wide Web Consortium (W3) was formed in late 1994 under the guidance of Tim Berners-Lee himself in an attempt to maintain some order and establish a stable core of standards for HTML by approving new developments, protocols, formats and extensions.[6]

Notwithstanding that this overview of the development and origins of the web is too brief and simplified, it does highlight one fundamental aspect which is essential for the content creator to grasp: namely that HTML was developed to be a device-independent document markup language and not a page description language such as PostScript. Its primary concern, to reiterate, above all was to facilitate the sharing of information across electronic networks regardless of platform and irregardless of how that information would ultimately be displayed at the users' ends. So it remains, in essence, today.

The creation of an intelligent user base – and the birth of a technophobic underclass

Once the architecture of the Internet was constructed, the elements that allowed the creation of the World Wide Web came into place, it seems, with relative ease, but that alone is not sufficient to explain the meteoric way that the medium has subsequently and so pervasively penetrated into mainstream life.

It is a truism, perhaps, to state that technological innovations and developments do not always lead where their creators originally intend. For indeed, if the system was originally envisaged as a means of sharing text-based information mainly between research, scientific and academic institutions and communities, then the development and evolution of the the smart web browser – and with it the vision of magazine-like pages combining text, images, even sound, animations, and video, that could be accessed by anyone in the world – enabled an otherwise fiendishly clever but heretofore closed system to excite the world at large, catching the attention and sparking the imagination of at once thousands and now millions of individuals, and eventually of the commercial and corporate worlds and their massive development budgets. Indeed, without the facility to entertain visually (so important to a generation weaned on television) as well as inform textually, then the World Wide Web might still be languishing in the dusty corridors and confines of academia.

Certainly the web browser has been instrumental to the continued evolution of the World Wide Web itself and to its phenomenal take up as a mass medium. But as for the process being led by the corporate world, quite the opposite has been the case. Companies have, in fact, been rather sluggish overall to embrace the potential of the web, not least because businessmen and accountants were, and to a large extent still are, hard pressed to see how they can make any money out of it. Sure, everyone is jumping on the bandwagon now, but make no mistake, the web has been a phenomenon that has mainly come from the grassroots up, and as much for this as for any other reason, it represents the most fundamental and cataclysmic shift to the publishing paradigm since Gutenberg.

Consider for a moment the opportunity that the web presents: without the need to buy any new or expensive equipment (most existing modern computers – five years old or less, say – are sufficient to a greater or lesser degree and the only extra hardware required is the modem, the little gizmo that links a computer to the telephone network, a relatively low-tech and inexpensive device) and without the need to invest time and energy in learning complicated computer programming skills (HTML is simply a text markup language that is easy to learn; you can gain proficiency in writing pure code in a few days), it has suddenly become possible to publish on the web, and not only that, but to publish and reach a potential global audience of millions at minimal cost.

At a stroke the World Wide Web has thus empowered everyone – anyone with computer access that is – to be a publisher and it is simply this sheer facility, I believe, that has led to the exponential creation, recreation, and procreation of web sites on such a remarkable scale. In the 8th WWW User Survey Report[7] by the Graphic, Visualization, & Usability Center (GVU) of Georgia Tech University, one of the most interesting findings is that some 46 per cent of respondents had 'created a web page' and that European respondents (67.66 per cent) were more likely to have created a web page than US respondents (43.42 per cent). While the GVU survey, which employs non-probabilistic sampling, may not be representative of web users in general, nonetheless, this link between web users as authors and publishers is, I believe, a significant one.

The origins of the web in academia, moreover, should by no means be underestimated. Much of the material on the web in the early days was already available in digital form, accessed on the Internet through other protocols (gopher, telnet and FTP). More significantly, the networking of academic and research institutions around the world, and the empowering of students and faculty to communicate with each other, friends, family and new acquaintances anywhere in the world through e-mail, has in a very short space of time created a mass intelligensia of potential content creators who not only know their way around the web but who have grown used to using it as a daily resource as naturally as using the library or the telephone.

Given that PC sales for the home market continue to increase at pace throughout the developed world (and certainly throughout Europe and the USA), and with new developments such as web TV already reality, with improvements in bandwidth, and the delivery of web services by fibre optic cable or satellite on the way, it is certain that the demographics of web access are evolving quickly, and the user base is expanding to an ever broader cross-section of society.

At the same time, however, it must be acknowledged that the phenomenon of the World Wide Web is undoubtedly creating a society of haves and have-nots, and this social divide is not just based on economics. The demographics of web use indicate that the so-called 'digital divide'[8] may have as much to do with age, gender and geography as disposable income, though undoubtedly the traditional underclasses of society lag some way behind the privileged.

Not everyone, by any means, considers that the prospect of a World Wide Web of universally accessible electronic information will be necessarily beneficial to society. Many fear the lack of any centralised control over content on the web, and point to the proliferation of obscene sites, as well as socially destructive sites that advocate racism, hatred, strange or obscure religious cults, or drug sub-cultures. Then there are those with ultraconservative and right wing agenda that are in favour of censorship of the web, and seek to silence legitimate organisations advocating gay, women's, or other minority rights and interests.

Philosophical issues are at stake, too. Social critic Neil Postman fears the creation of a new elite that will gain power over others simply through the mastery of the new technology, thus in the process leading to the creation of a technologically illiterate underclass.[9] In Sven Birkerts' eloquent and passionately written book, *The Gutenberg Elegies*,[10] he considers the prospect of a cyberworld of electronic publishing to represent an absolutely fundamental shift in our social and cultural values and is eager to assure that we are aware of what we are losing as we rush headlong towards a brave new world of electronic information that threatens to replace not just the physical book itself, but indeed the whole canon of western thought and belief as represented by the book. In the beginning, he seems to be reminding us, was the Word...

In such a brief space of time, the creation of the hard-wired, networked infrastructure that allows the the World Wide Web to function so miraculously, and the exponential proliferation of web sites that has followed, has already raised worrying and fundamental questions about content and the medium that delivers it.

1 Interestingly, the prototype of what today is known as the Internet was originally called the National Galactic Information Infrastructure, according to Barry M. Leiner. See article 'A Brief History of the Internet':
http://www.isoc.org/internet/history/brief.html
2 In *Being Digital,* Hodder & Stoughton 1995, Nicholas Negroponte distinguishes between transporting content in the form of atoms, that is manufactured print, and bits, electronic digital information. This simple distinction is one key to understanding the digital information age and all that it implies and promises.
3 Tim Berners-Lee, 1992, 'WWW Summary', W3 Consortium:
http://www.w3.org/Summary.html. This terse summary of the WWW project, written before the World Wide Web was fully accepted as a protocol, gives a fascinating insight into the origins of the phenomenon.
4 *Ibid.*
5 Ben Segal, 1995, 'A Short History of Internet Protocols at CERN',
http://wwwcn.cern.ch/pdp/ns/ben/TCPHIST.html
6 The web site of the World Wide Web Consortium (W3) is at once an important resource for new developments as well as an historic archive that documents the history and on-going evolution of the World Wide Web: http://www.w3.org
7 GVU's 8th WWW User Survey was run from 10 October 1997 through 16 November 1997 and was endorsed by the World Wide Web Consortium. A survey report is available at: http://gvu.gatech.edu/user_surveys/survey-1997-10/
8 Don Tapscott, writing about the 'net generation' in his book *Growing Up Digital*, McGraw -Hill 1998, refers to the 'digital divide' and ways to overcome it. See pp. 255-279. The book has its own on-going web site dedicated to the Net Generation: http://www.growingupdigital.com
9 See Neil Postman, 1993. *Technopoly The Surrender of Culture to Technology.* Vintage Books, New York. Interestingly, this book was written before the widescale take-up of the World Wide Web, but one sees many of Postman's fears being realised already.
10 Sven Birkerts, 1994. *The Gutenberg Elegies The Fate of Reading in an Electronic Age.* Faber and Faber, London.

CHAPTER TWO

Content on the Web

When Tim Berners-Lee originally set the World Wide Web in motion, the type of content that was being distributed over the new electronic networks was, most probably, inherently similar to that which had previously been distributed by other traditional means. It was the mode of delivery – the transmission of electronic digital bits as opposed to physical atoms – that was different, not the content itself. Whenever a new medium is created, the first content is inevitably carried over from other, older media.[1] What is most unpredictable, however, is the way new technology eventually can lead to changes and evolution in the very form and nature of content itself.

Certainly in its brief history, content on the web has already evolved and altered considerably, and is evolving still. Hand-in-hand with this process of evolution have been the progression of technological developments and innovations that have fueled it. The Mosaic browser, for example, was an early breakthrough as it allowed the integration of images with text (in the earliest web browsers, only text was able to be delivered). Netscape developed the user interface even further, as well as introducing a number of HTML extensions that at first only worked on Netscape browsers. The miracle of digitalisation, furthermore, has made possible real multimedia, with the facility to embed digital sound and video files in web sites (though until narrow bandwidth increases, multimedia is likely to remain more of a promise than a reality).

When Bill Gates decided that the Internet was where the future of Microsoft lay, he immediately grasped that the way to influence access to and content on the World Wide Web was naturally to supply and control the user interface by which means users access the web (just as he managed to achieve almost total market hegemony on the PC operating system through the successful implementation of the Microsoft computer user interface Windows in its various manifestations). He set out to achieve this by attempting to integrate a web browser into that same operating system, just as local area networking had been integrated within the Windows NT operating system environment. The web after all is but a global extension of local networking, and indeed it was its arch rival Netscape that first suggested that the web browser could even eventually replace the PC operating system and herald in the new generation of network computers.

Thus started the so-called 'browser wars': as Microsoft began to eat into the previous market domination of Netscape, allegations were made of unfair pressure put on computer manufacturers to include Microsoft's browser alongside its Windows operating system. Not surprisingly, the prospect of Bill Gates, the world's richest man, and his company Microsoft gaining domination not just over computer operating systems but the World Wide Web itself was a frightening one that eventually provoked the interest and concern of the United States Department of Justice, which began an investigation into Microsoft's alleged unfair practises. That prolonged case continues at the time of writing, and its outcome is by no means clear. But make no mistake: no less than the future of the form of the World Wide Web and the content we access is at stake.[2]

It is interesting, as I write this, to watch from the sidelines as the heavyweights continue to slug it out. Certainly over the past few years, Netscape and Microsoft Internet Explorer browser versions have appeared with frustrating regularity, each new offering loaded inevitably with more and more top heavy, memory hungry 'must have' features. Meanwhile other browser options continue to quietly emerge that offer more manageable, lightweight, and, most importantly fast-loading alternatives in the form of low memory browsers, some designed to function through a new generation of digital TV set-top boxes, proving that big may not always be best.[3] Indeed, the advent of web TV is one of the most significant developments that will have considerable impact on content and the form and shape of the web browser as web access makes the inevitable transition from office into living room.

What is certainly clear is that the web browser itself in great measure is the determinant of the shape and form of web content. To a large extent, this new medium has already achieved one aim of both Microsoft and Netscape: of establishing the web browser as the universal interface, replacing former desktop metaphors with a new visual vocabulary and way of navigating content that we are still groping to come to terms with. Not least is the problem that we have yet to define a common language that we all speak and understand: indeed, there can be as many ways of navigating web sites as there are site designers, since each site can in effect reinvent its own unique navigation system, with its own conventions, rules for hyperlinks, icons, structure and much else.

Certainly content on the web, its essential form and structure as well as the information or content itself that is so delivered, is evolving still, and given the decentralised and rather anarchic nature of the web, it is probable that no set conventions will in the short term at least become established, simply because part of the excitement of the medium is its very lack of them, and the granting of creative freedom to content creators and site designers alike, however frustrating this can be at times for the end user, who is often overlooked within the whole process.

Looking back, for example, first generation web sites were mainly concerned with the functional presentation of information as delivered through what we now would consider super-slow transmission rates, often to be viewed on monochrome monitors displaying text-only browsers. Early HTML was only able to describe the structure of a document not its appearance and as a result little thought was given to layout or design; such sites, with their grey backgrounds, edge-to-edge text, blank lines and horizontal rules, often tried to present material in a flat, linear fashion that resulted in long lists of menus but with little creative structure or thought given to the arrangement and navigation of the hypertext documents.

As new visual features were added, the look of web sites certainly altered considerably through the addition of tiled backgrounds, creative typography (produced as bit-mapped images), the addition of animations, the arrangement of text in tables to create multi-column layouts, the incorporation of new extensions to HTML, and the facility to navigate through the use of tables and frames. The latest web sites now make use of concepts such as visual metaphors to guide visitors and aid navigation, while improvements in browser features, the development of HTML 4.0 that includes among other innovations cascading style sheets which enable greater control over layout and presentation, and technological developments such as Shockwave (allowing the import and integration of Macromedia Director movies and Flash animations), java and javascript, streaming audio and video have all had considerable impact on the shape, form, and appearance of content on the web today.

Yet, while there is no sign that either the development of the web browser or the creation of new technological innovations will slow down, thus ensuring that content on the web as we know it even now is set to continue to evolve, it is probably true to say that certain elements which differentiate content on the web from content in other media are now firmly established.

Non-linear hypertext

One of the most fundamental and significant features of web content is that it is essentially non-linear. The concept of hypertext, that is, of text that can be linked to other text, was inherent in the original conception of the World Wide Web and this has been extended to relate to multimedia hypertext whereby the links can be graphics, movies, or sound files as well as text. Non-linear hypertext means that it is the web site visitor who chooses what threads of an argument or document to explore or pursue, not the content creator. Inherent within this is the concept of active and interactive exploration, a powerful process that can certainly aid in communicating ideas effectively and with a different impact than sequentially organised linear texts.

More fundamentally, the effective use of hypertext results in the grouping, interconnecting and separating of ideas to result in a structure that may be horizontal, vertical, or seemingly at random. Indeed, the power of the hyperlink allows a web site to extend even beyond its own limits, since it makes no difference (and sometimes the visitor is not even aware) whether such links refer to internal 'pages' within the same web site or else to external web pages located on servers anywhere else in the world.

Thus a web site may have multiple doorways of entry and exit. By its very non-linear nature, a web site does not usually have a fixed order in which it must be visited. The act of accessing a web site, therefore, becomes something of a serendipitous act of exploration and discovery that is unique to each visitor, who moves through the site in whatever order he/she cares to, and perhaps even moves outside the document to an external document and never comes back. Similarly, the point of entry into a document may be through that document's Home or Welcome page; or else it may be through a link to a page buried deep within the web site, made by some other external web site that the creator does not even know exists.

Just as the process of web site content creation is altered by the form and structural options that hypertext presents, so does this form and structure have considerable impact on the very act of reading. To some this can indeed be liberating; others, though, may prefer the order that sequential texts necessarily impose on the presentation of information.

Many-to-many publishing model

Another fundamental difference that content on the web has over traditional media content is that due to its potentially ubiquitous distribution, the publishing model has altered from the broadcasting paradigm of one-to-many to a 'narrowcasting' model of many-to-many. The high production and delivery costs of television, book, newspaper and magazine publishing traditionally resulted in relatively small numbers of projects that sought to attract as large an audience as possible.[4] The web, on the other hand, has the real potential to have as many publishers as visitors and viewers. In this sense, it has certainly already proved to be one of the most powerful media for self-publishing as well as for niche or boutique publishing to highly targeted, special-interest audiences, no matter how small.

The form and types of web sites that have been and are being created certainly reflect this. The Home page has emerged as a new literary form in its own right as individuals from all over the world make their mark in cyberspace by publishing documents about themselves, their professional and personal interests, anything at all that they want to say. Indeed, as a forum for self-expression, for artistic experimentation, for ranting and raving at injustice, for freedom of expression, and for making political statements, the web provides an outlet with the potential to reach global audiences who would otherwise be impossible to bring together. Indeed, the latter point is of more than minor significance.

For the web's power and potential as an instrument of free speech should not be underestimated, and in the past year, we've seen examples of how it is has been used to promote the causes and ideals of the oppressed and disaffected in Mexico, Indonesia, Kosovo and elsewhere. In China dissidents exchange and publish information over the Internet that would otherwise be suppressed, and seek to use the new media to find means and ways to communicate and create communities of those with shared values, though government officials may seek to find ways to censor and control such conduits of communication and information dissemination. This may not be that easy to achieve: Mao said that power comes out of the barrel of a gun, but in fact, today it may be those cyber-revolutionaries who are able to wield a computer keyboard effectively that are most effective and irritating to authoritarian and oppressive regimes.

A significant side-effect of the shift from the top-down, one-to-many to the many-to-many broadcasting model that the web represents is the inevitable loss of a common national culture and canon. Indeed, as the world divides into ever smaller and smaller units through electronic publishing that the web and other digital broadcasting media (such as digital and satellite TV, with their plethora of channels) represent, there is an inevitable loss of national vocabulary and experiences that are common to all as part of our common culture. The days when you knew, for example, that everyone was or would be watching the same TV show on a Sunday night, and talking about it the next day in the office or pub, may well now be gone for good as we each to each, in front of our glowing computer monitors and web TVs, confront and explore our own personal agenda and special interests. Even within the unit of the nuclear family, it is likely that individual members will pursue their own interests independently: the days even when the family all sat around the 'box' together are probably long gone. Is this loss of common shared experience through national media a matter of concern, or should it be?

Interactivity and push technology

Perhaps one of the most significant and revolutionary aspects about content on the web is its potential for interactivity, the prospect of content creators for the first time ever able to have real time or asynchronous dialogues with their visitors through chat, e-mail or other interactive experiences. This is achieved in many ways. The easiest is simply by having an e-mail link whereby visitors can correspond with the content creator, asking questions, offering feedback, and in the process creating a dialogue between publisher and reader. Many web sites have guest books where they invite comments and indeed this can lead to a dialogue not simply between the content creator and visitor but furthermore between the visitors themselves.[5]

Content on the web enables, even demands, feedback from the web user, and this adds a powerful tool to the content creator. From a commercial point of view, certainly, it furthermore suggests a new business model that the web makes possible whereby a company is able to build personal one-to-one relationships with its visitors through interactive dialogue.

The use of intelligent log statistics analysis tools[6] can give the content creator a precise idea of the demographics of its actual audience. Such statistics can be revealing in the extreme, giving indications about where visitors are from, the time of day they accessed the site, whether from work or home, the type and version of browser used, how and from where they came to the site, how long they stayed and what pages they spent most time on. It would not be possible, or only at the most exhorbitant expense, for a magazine or newspaper publisher or a television producer to gather such precise facts and market research about its actual audience; the knowledge so gained is potentially of considerable value to the content creator in matching content to the needs of the audience most precisely. (It is also worrying from the user's point of view that companies in particular can gain such detailed information about them and their browsing habits; but privacy is another issue that is looked at later in this book.)

Any form of publishing, of course, should consider its audience's needs and desires. Writing that is undertaken simply for the writer's own satisfaction is often self-indulgent and rarely successful. The web, on the other hand, provides the opportunity to turn this basic presumption on its head through the development of so-called push technology. Push technology empowers the reader not the content creator to determine the delivery of the content that he/she so desires or anticipates. The need for such information filters is indeed a pressing one considering the literally millions of web sites at each user's disposal to choose from. Push technology works by allowing a user to determine those subjects that he/she is interested in, then for remote spider robots to harvest and deliver that content in some sort of ordered and structured form.

Take, for example a daily newspaper. Most of us have neither the time nor the inclination to read such quotidian offerings from front to back in their entirety. We might peruse the main home news stories, then turn to the sports pages, read the book reviews, obituaries, or classified ads. On the other hand, we might never even glance at the financial pages, women's features, or editorial pages. Using push technology, a custom electronic newspaper can be threaded together that would serve our needs most precisely – and be delivered to our electronic desktops at eight in the morning, rain or shine. Though this would undoubtedly be a more time-effective document than the whole, unwieldy broadsheet newspaper, however, the intangible pleasure of serendipitously leafing through a paper, pausing to browse articles that one did not even know you had an interest in, might inevitably be lost (though there are, in theory, ways of adding a random story selection element to the custom construction of such pushed content).

Is the use of push technology a model for the future? Interestingly, at the present time, it appears not. Widely touted as the 'killer application' of 1997, push seems to have singularly failed to capture the imagination of the web surfing public. Internet Explorer 4's attempt to put push technology on the web browser interface in the form of channels customised to suit each user has not been deemed a great success, not least, it seems because the broadcasting metaphor implies the passive receipt of content inherent in the old one-to-many broadcasting model. Web surfers, on the other hand, conditioned to searching for material, and addicted to the thrill of finding it by whatever means – the use of search engines, electronic bulletin boards and the like – prefer, it seems, an active not a passive web experience, a fact that content creators should well bear in mind. Whether or not, as the web moves from the office into couch-potato land, i.e. the living room, users' expectations and capacities actively to explore will alter remains to be seen in coming years and will certainly be interesting to monitor.

Multimedia and the web

The miracle of digital technology means that web sites can truly be all singing and dancing through the use of sound, video, animations and virtual reality environments. The limiting factor at the moment is narrow bandwidth; sound and video files in particular can take up huge amounts of space, even for brief clips, and it is this more than barriers in the technology itself that has kept true multimedia off most of the web at the current time. This, however, must be set to change radically. Streaming technology, for example, even now facilitates the delivery of sound and video clips that play as they download, a process that greatly speeds up the effective use of such elements on web pages.[7] Streaming audio can be used for real time broadcasts of music, while streaming video is used by news teams such as CNN. As new means are found to deliver greater bandwidth, then the possibility of delivering even full-length movies on demand over the web could become reality not just a promise.

At times, though, we must ask, is it all worth it, worth the desperate struggle, the downloading of plug-ins and helper applications, the inevitable crashes and system freezes, just to get that tiny, in real time (but so huge in digital bits) clip? Certainly the use of existing multimedia technologies for the delivery of news stories as they break provides an alternative medium that is especially useful for those who cannot get to a TV or radio, while the interactive possibilities of communicating with the audience to get their instant feedback means that such web sites can offer more than simply a replication of traditional media content. But the ease of using them, even with a relatively high end set-up and a fast modem or ISDN connection, is still far from seamless, in my experience. Indeed if you want sound and video for your news or sport, then why make things overly complicated: just switch on the radio or TV.

Multimedia of course is part of the web and it would be foolish to deny it. Some of the most creative effects, however, come not simply from the delivery of audio or video, which still may be done by traditional media much more effectively and cheaply, but from technologies developed specifically for new media. Macromedia Director movies delivered by means of Shockwave[8] can provide some astounding interactive special effects, while the use of java applets and javascripts, two related new media technologies that allow for platform independent delivery of applications and special effects without the need for plug-ins, is beginning to bring real life and interactivity to the web.

Content creation versus content distribution

Before the World Wide Web, the activities of content creation and content distribution remained, though obviously intrinsically linked, nonetheless very different and separate ones, the former the provenance of the author, the latter of the publisher. The web, on the other hand, has liberated content creation from content distribution, and brings together the activities of author and publisher, with huge implications for content creation. Indeed if, as already stressed, every author can be his/her own publisher on the web, so can every publisher be his/her own author, as evidenced by the rise and rise of the personal Home page.

There are a number of implications that this conjunction of content creation and content distribution brings to the fore. One of the most pressing is its ramification on integrity, value and authority of content. When the number of authors/publishers threatens to exceed the number of readers/viewers, then there is a certain risk that the web's facility for self-publishing leads to an information overload where the web user is left unable to distinguish the authoritative and useful from the rambling, self-indulgent, the dross, the content that is of no interest or merit to any but, perhaps (and it is a big perhaps) the creator's own mother.

The high costs of production and distribution of traditional media, by contrast, has had the effect of a certain degree of self-regulation in as much as the most blatant rubbish does not see the light of day simply because it is not considered commercially viable to publish it (though that is not to say that volumes of rubbish have not been, or will not continue to be, published and broadcast). Moreover, the very fact of being published, something that traditionally has not been easy to accomplish, confers a certain *de facto* authority both to the author or content creator as well as to the content itself. Editorial trust and authority between author and reader is furthermore often safeguarded by the guarantee and reputation that lies behind a well known publishing imprint.[9]

On the web, such assurances may be harder to find, at least for the present time. In a medium that seems almost actively to encourage the dissemination of false information, and the adoption of new roles and identities, there can be consequently something of a crisis in confidence or faith in information that is delivered across such electronic networks. Material accessed from a bona fide and authoritative site may appear identical to that produced by some fly-by-night or even downright irresponsible operation or organisation. How to distinguish between the two?

The search for new economic models

An answer may come about in part through the development of new economic models for content creators and providers on the web. Indeed, while the web has liberated content provision from content distribution, it has left as a huge void adequate business models for financing such electronic publishing initiatives. In the past, the basic business models for publishing and broadcasting were either for a publisher to produce a product, say a book, and then recoup costs as well as make a profit through selling it, or else to produce a product, say a magazine or newspaper, and recoup costs and make a profit both by selling it as well as by selling advertising. The revenues from the latter in many cases have traditionally been of considerably higher value than the revenues generated from sales. Commercial TV broadcasters have traditionally offered programmes to the audience for free in return for the attention and audience figures that they could offer to advertisers or so-called 'sponsors'. The advent of satellite and cable broadcasting as well as digital TV changed that basic broadcasting model by charging subscriptions to the viewer in return for content. Some go so far as to charge a subscription for content, levy additional pay-per-view fees on a programme-by-programme basis, and submit the viewer to advertising to boot!

On the web, such business models may be hardly relevant. Service providers have attempted to become content providers by developing their own list of proprietary services and content available to their own subscribers only (the model followed by CompuServe, MSN, AOL and others), but the value of such content is undoubtedly diminished by the overwhelming amount of content on similar subjects that is at present available on the World Wide Web for free. At the time of writing, the provision of content on a subscription only basis is not yet developed, though certain sites do successfully charge for access to material.[10]

As new forms of electronic cash evolve, especially forms that facilitate micro-transactions (charging say one pence for a page each time it is accessed, to be debited automatically from a user's cyber-bank account), then the business model of charging the web user directly for content may become more widespread and viable. The provision of content then would return to its basic business model whereby that which is economically successful is deemed to be that which is most authoritative, entertaining, informational or whatever. If information is power, and power is money, then inevitably sites that continue to offer content for free would conversely come to be considered of lesser value than the established 'brands' that charge for it. However, for the time being at any rate, it looks as if content will on the whole continue to be accessible free on most of the web.

If electronic publishers cannot sell their content, then they will have to seek to sell their audience. The year 1997 saw a significant rise in banner advertising on web sites (banner adverts are advertisements that are placed on third-party web sites which attract attention and, when clicked, take the visitor to the advertisor's site). This trend looks set to continue as multi-national corporations and small businesses alike are beginning to incorporate the web into their overall marketing strategies. Indeed, companies that have invested considerably in web site creation as a means of self-promotion need to find ways to drive visitors to their sites. Banner advertisements that link to a company's site can indeed be an effective means of achieving this, and one that can be measureable, too. Many sites that accept adverts charge advertisers per click, that is not simply for the number of potential viewers who might see a banner advert, but for the number who actually and positively act by clicking to visit the advertiser's intended destination.

Sponsorship of web sites is another new means of funding content provision, as is membership of a site by subscription, and the sale of spin-off goods, services or products. Another interesting new model is that of hybrid publishing whereby a web site is used to tie in with other media, perhaps the sale of a book or magazine, or a cross-link to a television programme or movie.

But while all these business models promise a way to gain returns on the creation of content, none have yet proved to be entirely effective. 'Word' and 'Charged', two early and groundbreaking webzines launched in 1995 and published by Icon CMT Corp., eventually foundered. 'Word', a culture and arts zine and 'Charged', a sports zine, were ambitious electronic publishing projects that hoped to gain revenue from advertising, but this proved difficult to sustain. Perhaps they were simply before their time.

'Slate',[11] meanwhile, published by Microsoft, began on 9 March 1998 to charge a $19.95 subscription for the magazine-style e-zine, even though its publishers have accepted that this will result in a significant drop in readership. But early indications, say the company, are promising.[12] Interestingly, Microsoft plans furthermore to offer a 60 page hard copy edition of the e-zine for sale to those without web access or who simply want to browse the publication in print, an indication that crossover from old media to new works in reverse too and that traditional outlets still offer ways of reaching audiences not possible exclusively through the web.

The economics of financing content provision clearly remains in its infancy, but what is certain is that new models are being tried and tested and it is certain that in the near future successful means will have been found to enable content providers and electronic publishers to be rewarded for their efforts and for web users to be able to find and access sites that they can have confidence in.

Information filters

It is interesting to note that the web sites that are most popular, receiving literally millions of hits a day,[13] are search directories and robot search engines such as Yahoo!, Excite, Infoseek, Alta Vista, Lycos and others. Indeed, it is difficult to imagine the development of the web as a mass medium without the development of the search directory. How often we all turn to them as a means of finding sites on whatever subject we happen to be interested in or merely just thinking about in passing; how essential search directories have come to be as a tool to help us survive the ever-present risk of being subsumed by information overload. Search directories exist to filter content, to categorise it, indeed even to rank it (simply by means of which sites come up top of a search list) in order to make it easier for us to find what we are looking for. As such, they represent a new model of metacontent – content about content – that serves to filter information and content in order to make it easier for us to access it.

Of course, no search engine or directory is comprehensive; not only is the web evolving at too fast a rate for any to keep up with everything, moreover, each has its own criteria for sites included and for order of ranking, as well as its own means of registration and category selection. The sheer overwhelming number of hits per day of the most popular sites is an indication of the extent that web users have come to rely on the search engine. The need for such information filters is clearly pressing but is our reliance, based in part on laziness, in part on ignorance, in fact an active encouragement to the propagation of this parasitical form of content?

There has been recently a profusion of web sites that are simply compilations of other web sites, organised and categorised to suit the individual user, but created with the addition of no original information or content whatsoever. Indeed, it is rather like constructing a series of robust wooden frames that display paintings or photographs produced by someone else and taking credit for originating the material yourself. The search directories themselves are in many cases most well placed to create such metacontent. My Yahoo!,[14] for example, is a personalised compilation of sites and stories compiled from a variety of sources and news agencies – Reuters, Press Association and others – that change regularly throughout the day and night depending on what each user has indicated interest in. My Yahoo! doesn't actually create the stories, it just compiles them from other sources according to each individual user's specified interests and preferences.

The basic and fundamental concept of hyperlinking, both to other external sites as well as encouraging sites to give reciprocal links in return, certainly encourages a culture of sharing of content that enables such custom content to be created. But it may be open to abuse, raise questions of intellectual property rights, and give rise to the creation of sites that are little more than compilations plagiarised from others.

Yet information filters clearly serve a need on the web. As already mentioned, the web is notoriously error-plagued, and there is much information that has been published that may be misleading or even downright incorrect. Sites that rate other sites, therefore, can assist in helping to distinguish those that are worth visiting. For example, in the field of nutrition, there is a plethora of sites purporting to offer good eating advice, but not all are reliable, while in other cases there may be a hidden corporate agenda that makes such information subjective at best. Tuft University's School of Nutrition Science and Policy has created and launched the 'Nutrition Navigator',[15] which serves to rate nutrition-related web sites on a 25 point scale, with the heaviest weighting going to accuracy of information. This is a worthwhile filtering service that is to be applauded, for it indeed helps users to distinguish the cyber-bogus from the genuinely useful.

Can we always trust the raters, however? There is no such thing as total objectivity on the web, or in any other media, and any form of rating is by nature selective and subjective. What, for example, about sites that serve to filter material deemed suitable for children: what is the criteria employed and can we ever be sure that it is reliable? Or those that purport to exclude offensive adult material but block responsible sites catering for, say, the gay and lesbian communities? Or sites that filter alcohol and tobacco related sites as of potential harm but in the process ban sites relating to wine producing regions and wine travel? And can we be certain that those offering a radical right wing agenda (or radical left wing for that matter) have not taken control of such filters? Indeed, this issue is of considerable importance and the politics of filtering is discussed in a later chapter of this book, in particular as it relates to freedom of information and censorship.

The web and other publishing media

As new models for the economic development of electronic publishing on the web evolve, as the web continues to develop at pace and new web sites appear at alarming rate, there will be an inevitable impact on other publishing media. New opportunities are certainly being created, but are traditional publishers in a position to take advantage of them? Indeed, is it even desirable that traditional publishers and broadcasters become the creators of new media content in the future?

Book publishers have the chance to make use of hybrid publishing whereby web sites are used as marketing tools that amplify knowledge, increase exposure, and encourage books to be purchased. Take for example, Dorling Kindersley, the British publisher that pioneered a range of books with a unique visual style and appeal that ranges across disciplines and subjects, from cookery to reference to travel guides to childrens' books. The company web site[16] is geared mainly towards children and combines multimedia, including creative and exciting Macromedia Shockwave movies and animations that truly bring books and CDs, such as the outstanding Dinosaur Hunter, to life. Many other publishers have in recent years realised the added value that a good web site can add as a marketing tool for books, and indeed it is interesting to note that Amazon.com,[17] described as 'Earth's biggest bookstore' has proved to be one of the most effective outlets for e-commerce on the web. Indeed, book publishers should take note: rather than fear that book sales could decline as more and more information becomes available on the web, the runaway success of Amazon is an indication of the huge potential of the web as an aid to traditional marketing and sales of books.

Newspaper and magazine publishers have not been slow to look at repurposing existing content for the web, either. From tiny specialised niche publications to the mainstream glossies, there are electronic magazines and newspapers on virtually every topic under the sun and stars. Custom e-zines specially designed and created for new media have demonstrated that a significant readership can be established for new on-line content. It is interesting to note that one model that newspaper and magazine publishers utilise in web content is that of regular daily, weekly, monthly or quarterly 'issues' whereby the entire – or almost all of the content on the site is refreshed or renewed regularly, with previous issues archived electronically.[18] Certainly, for web sites to be effective, it is essential that the material changes regularly and is kept timely and up-to-date, and this model is one way of achieving this.

At the moment, small and large publishers are competing on a relatively even playing field, and indeed the low or no budget enthusiast can compete with big spenders in the corporate publishing world. But it is probable that eventually money will speak loudest in the end and the inevitable marketing process of creating premium brands that attract all the revenue (from whatever source) will win out. Indeed, as the web matures, as users become conditioned to accessing it as easily and routinely as they access other traditional media, it seems likely that the heavy promotional budgets of the largest web publishers will hold sway and influence over the low or no budget sites, whatever the relative value and worth of content. Is it too much to hope that web users, accustomed to thinking and searching for themselves and to getting web content for free, may resist this corporate trend?

Television and radio similarly have come to new media as a means of enhancing and adding value to their existing content. One of the most impressive examples is the BBC,[19] which uses its on-line web site as a comprehensive vehicle for information about most of its services and activities, including national television programmes, radio, education, news, world service, regional broadcasts, weather and much else. Television programmes can link up with the web site and provide, for example, real chat forums that allow viewers the opportunity to discuss issues with presenters or producers. The history program 'Walden on Heroes' was linked with a real chat forum on the BBC Education web site that allowed viewers the chance to question the former 'Weekend World' presenter Brian Walden live on-line about his notions of heroism. When Gordon Brown, Chancellor of the Exchequer, presented his annual Budget to the nation on 17 March 1998, the BBC News web site[20] provided both on-line live video coverage of the speech (from BBC 1 television) as well as web audio coverage (from Radio 4 and 5). The BBC's familiar 'Budget Day' personality Peter Snow presented a virtual community 'Budget Town' with an interactive map that used advanced multimedia technology based on Shockwave. ITN, meanwhile, not to be outdone, made use of the interactive capabilities of the web to field questions both before and after the Budget by e-mail, coordinating and presenting the answers both on TV as well as on-line.

Such synergetic uses of the web together with traditional media certainly are examples of how the new media can be used to add considerable value to traditional media products and indeed be instrumental in shaping opinion and even shaping events and news, or at least our perception of them.

Just as traditional media is looking forward to the challenge of new media, so, at the same time, does that new media itself still look to older traditional publishing models for shape and structure. E-zines have as their inspiration the low-budget, often self-published fanzines of popular culture. Electronic newspapers and magazines often try to take on the journalistic design appearance of their paper equivalents, even though they really aren't magazines at all in the sense of how most of us understand the word. And the use of channels as a web metaphor comes from television and suggests a broadcasting model of new content continuously playing and on tap to an audience that can tune in whenever and wherever.

Meanwhile, a new form of content that is unique to the medium begins to take shape and emerge. We see this process unfold before our very eyes and it is nothing less than fascinating to watch. When a major news story like the Clinton/Lewinsky affair broke in early 1998, for example, the story was driven by reports published first on the World Wide Web. Lewinsky, an intern at the White House, was alleged to have had a sexual relationship with President Clinton, an affair that he strenuously and vigorously denied. *Newsweek* magazine originally had details of the alleged affair but spiked the story. However, Matt Drudge,[21] a notorious cybergossip, spread the rumour on his web site, the Drudge Report on 17 January and it quickly became the hottest national news story around. The rest is history.

As claims and counterclaims have subsequently flown wildly across all media, this example has enabled us to consider some of the more obvious advantages and disadvantages of new media and traditional media. For speed of delivery the web can even rival 24 hour news broadcasting such as CNN, providing a forum for instant updates of news events as they happen. The web offers virtually unlimited space, so stories as in-depth as can be imagined and as spurious and irrelevant can be posted or published. Traditional media by contrast is limited by time (TV's scheduled broadcasting slots) or physical space (the number of pages of a publication). As a profusion of web sites have spawned on the back of the Lewinsky affair, many created by amateurs, the low delivery costs of web publishing are apparent: this is a medium that requires no print, no delivery trucks, no newsagents or TV studios, no editorial offices, so anyone wanting to pitch in her or his two cents can freely do so. The web, unlike other media, is interactive, and real time chat rooms, newsgroups, and usenet discussion forums offer an 'instant soap box' for any and all to share their opinions.[22] And of course this is a medium that is open for business 24 hours as access is universal and ubiquitous for those who are on-line.

When Judge Hiller Zobel announced that he would give his decision on the Louise Woodward[23] case over the Internet, that fact was hailed as an unprecedented, newsworthy event in itself. Not only was it deemed to be a method that would get the decision to as many people as possible in the quickest fashion, it was also deemed to be a method that allowed the delivery of content without intermediation and the bias that inevitably comes through interpretation by the press.

Certainly both the Lewinsky and Woodward affairs are evidence of the power of the web as a publishing medium as well as a medium that can influence, even create news and events. When America's Health Network decided to broadcast on 16 June 1998[24] the first live childbirth on the World Wide Web, it further demonstrated some of the advantages of this new medium. Though childbirth has been broadcast before on television, the medium of the web in theory allowed the event to be shown unedited and in real time, as it actually happened and for however long the event would take; AHN, a cable television channel, chose the web over TV because of the uncertainties over how long the birth would last meant that it would interfere with programme scheduling. As it turned out, the webcast itself proved to be something of a stillbirth: though baby Sean was successfully delivered, the feeble current limitations of bandwidth meant that global interest in the event caused the server to crash and few were able to witness the historic moment. Furthermore, the quality of the webcast, using streaming video, left much to be desired (though I can't confirm this as I was not able to access the site at all). Nonetheless, technological problems notwithstanding, the webcast certainly points the way to the future and demonstrates the power of the new medium.

Of course, Alvin Toffler predicted the end of newspapers more than 20 years ago in his book *Future Shock* and many futurologists believe that old traditional media will ultimately, and sooner rather than later, give way to new digital media. That is still probably some time away. Every medium has certain advantages and disadvantages and the new and innovative need not replace the previous incumbents. Television superseded the wireless, but radio remains as popular and valid a medium as ever. As for the web, TV is still more immediate and gives far higher quality for visual treatment, while newspapers have authority, credibility and portability that new media lacks. There are other less tangible factors, too. Newspapers fill a social need in our lives, providing common points of reference that allows us as readers to connect with those who share our points of view and values. They provide us with common experiences that we discuss during the day and they reflect our collective mindsets and perceptions of events. Readers of *The Daily Telegraph* undoubtedly have a different view on the world than readers of *The Guardian* or *The Daily Express*. A similar important social role is still carried out by national broadcasters such as the BBC. On the web, though, there are as yet no web sites comprehensive or commonly visited enough to fufill such a social role.

Clearly new media is not going to replace old traditional media. What is apparent, however, is that new media is shaping itself through the influence of old media while those older forms themselves are having to adapt to life in the electronic age of information: witness the fact that so many TV programmes and movies now have their own web sites as a matter of course. It seems certain that new forms of content will continue to emerge – new media and hybrid forms based on combinations of new and traditional – whether created or repurposed by traditional publishers or by new media specialists that have come to the web from totally different backgrounds.

The ultimate shape of those forms of content on the web, however, is and will continue to be determined by the interface design that is the boundary between our horizons and those of the cyber-universe beyond.

1 Marshall McLuhan, in his media studies classic, *Understanding Media*, first published in 1964, considers how technology and content interact: 'The first two centuries of printing from moveable types were motivated much more by the desire to see ancient and medieval books than by the need to read and write new ones.' p. 171.

2 AOL's merger with Netscape, announced in November 1998, has upped the stakes, bringing together Netscape's browser, the user interface, with AOL's considerable user base and existing proprietary content.

3 Alternative browsers worth checking out (some are freely available) include: Lynx (available from http://www.lynx.browser.org); Mosaic (available from http://www.ncsa.uiuc.edu/SDG/Software/Mosaic/); Opera (available from http://www.operasoftware.com); and Tango (available from http://www.alis.com).

4 Small numbers being relative, notwithstanding the high numbers of books published in Great Britain, the scores of established and newly launched magazines and newspapers, and the large number of television programmes originated each year.

5 The Mile End Park, an inner London urban renewal project funded in part by the Millennium Commission webcast live on the web on 4 March 1998 to gain feedback from local residents, schoolchildren and park planners around the world, using the interactive technology of the web to help shape and change actual physical space:http://www.mileendpark.co.uk

6 Such as those offered by companies like WebTrends: http://www.webtrends.com

7 To use these features, it is necessary to configure helper applications in a browser's plug-in folder, such as RealAudio's RealPlayer. For further information, go to: http://www.realaudio.com

8 Macromedia Shockwave is a compression technology that facilitates the delivery of Macromedia Director movies and Macromedia Flash animations. It has become one of the industry standards on creative web sites. To view such 'shockwaved' files, however, you need to download the relevant plug-in from the Macromedia web site: http://www.macromedia.com

9 Vanity publishing, by contrast, whereby an author has paid to manufacture and publish his/her own book, has long been considered the last resort for the unpublishable – and by extension unworthy – authors. This scorn for the self-published author has not been carried over onto the web as visitors to web sites seem particularly unconcerned about the need to validate a content creator's credentials or credibility.

10 The New York Times 'TimesFAX', for example, is now available by subscription only in PDF (Adobe Portable Document Format), though the electronic daily is still available for free: http://www.nytimes.com. The 'Wall Street Journal Online' is similarly fee-based, while the popular ESPN 'SportsZone' charges for some features. Probably the most successful subscription-only sites are the scores of pornographic and sex sites that have done little to edify the reputation of content on the web.

11 Slate: http://www.slate.com

12 Michael Kinsley, Slate's editor reported, 'As of this writing, two weeks after we

began accepting credit cards, about 10,000 subscribers have signed up. In a world where a formidable institution like the Wall Street Journal has 180,000-plus paying online subscribers more than a year after it started charging, and where Playboy's site is considered a success at 22,000 subscribers, we're pretty pleased that 10,000 people signed up before they even had to. Our goal is to have 15,000 to 20,000 subscribers within the first few months.'Slate, 6/3/98
http://www.slate.com/Readme/98-03-07/Readme.asp
13 Internet research firm RelevantKnowledge Inc., according to a Reuters article published on Jan. 12th, 1998, reported that "more than 16.7 'unique' users travelled last month [Dec. 1997] to http://www.yahoo.com where they accessed Yahoo!'s search engine", making it the most visited domain on the World Wide Web for that period.
14 My Yahoo! can be configured and personalised for individual users by going to: http://www.my.yahoo.com and selecting My Yahoo! from the menu.
15 Nutrition Navigator: http://www.navigator.tufts.edu/
16 Dorling Kindersley: http://www.dk.com
17 Amazon.com is one of the success stories of e-commerce on the web. It claims to have over 1.5 million customers: http://www.amazon.com
18 An interesting electronic e-zine worth checking out is 'Urban Desires', a cutting edge site with creative design and content. This electronic publication first appeared in December 1994 and thus, by studying the archive issues, it is possible to trace the development not only of the publication but of the web and web interface design itself: http://www.desires.com/
19 BBC On-line: http://www.bbc.co.uk. One of the most interesting and successful corporate consumer sites in Britain is 'Beeb@the BBC': http://www.beeb.com.
20 BBC News: http://www.bbc.co.uk/news/
21 Matt Drudge has come to personify the struggle between freedom of information and the need for responsible standards of journalism on the Internet. Considered by some an irresponsible right-wing muckraker, and championed by others as a pioneering newshound that takes on the establishment, Drudge, even to those who do not support his politics, is undoubtedly one of the leading proponents of disintermediated content, and as such is a champion of free speech on the Internet. Matt Drudge's web site, The Drudge Report, is at: http://www.drudgereport.com
22 A late-breaking development, as this book was in its production stages (January 1999), is that President Clinton was impeached and due to stand trial in the US Senate. Individual citizens, fed up with the whole impeachment process, established a web site – http://www.MoveOn.org – to register their protest, and as of 8 January 1999, this had already attracted some 450,000 supporters who collectively pledged some $10 million dollars to the cause. This is an example of how the medium is

being used to empower individual citizens to voice their grievances against those in power who they feel are acting against their wishes.

23 Woodward, a British nanny, was accused and found guilty of the second degree murder of Matthew Eapen, a baby in her care. The public outcry at the jury's decision provoked Judge Zobel to reconsider the case, and, after due deliberation he overturned the jury's decision, changing the verdict to manslaughter and freeing the young woman on appeal. Judge Zobel's decision was due to be released on the Internet, but it is ironic that a power failure just one minute before court officials were due to send Zobel's decision by e-mail to waiting news organisations caused the system to break down. Thus, though the computers were back up and running again in less than an hour and the decision was duly posted on the web, by then most of the news organisations had received it by old fashioned technology, using paper and fax.

24 The first live birth on the Internet, by mother Elizabeth of baby Sean, took place on 16 June 1998. The broadcast of the delivery was unedited and in real time and used streaming video technology, but such were the demands on the server that the system could not cope and few of the expectant global audience could access it. The site can be accessed at America's Health Network:
http://www.AHN.com/livebirth/index.htm

CHAPTER THREE

Putting the Best Interface Forward

I f the desktop personal computer is the the interface – that point or intersection through which we communicate and by which means we gain access – to the Internet, then it is undoubtedly a clumsy and unwieldy one. Those neo-Luddites who cry that the end of the book (and the world) is nigh need probably not fear cyber-Armageddon just yet, for we are still a long way from coming up with an alternative that we can curl up in bed with.[1]

Undoubtedly the way we access the web is heavy handed and clumsy, the interface between ourselves and the universe of cyberspace still by no means a seamless one. Surely, in years to come, we shall look back in gentle and forgiving amusement at the great lengths that we have had to go to, the hoops and intertwined hoops we've jumped through in these early and formative years in our efforts to gain access to the web: the connection through the desktop PC, essentially an office machine; the unwieldy and crude interfaces; the interminably slow download speeds over primitive analogue modems; the wait; the system crashes; the frustration; the excitement and sheer thrill of it all!

Any interface that makes the user aware of itself is probably an unsuccessful one, or at the least one that is less successful or effective than that which works seamlessly and unnoticed in the background. The World Wide Web is an incredibly complicated technological marvel and I don't profess even vaguely to understand its inner workings. Nor do I understand the workings of telecommunications that allows me to pick up an object on my desk, punch in a few numbers, and speak with anyone, anywhere on earth who is in range of a similar object: the telephone. For that matter, I've never remotely understood how radio waves make their way to me from hundreds or even thousands of miles away in order to reach the box in my room that plays music or tells me the news. And anyway, do we need to understand such inner workings? In the case of the telephone or the radio, the technologies that drive them have become so ingrained in our daily lives as to be virtually invisible. We are only reminded of them when foul weather causes interference with our reception, or brings down a telephone line.

The web, on the other hand, is by no means seamlessly integrated into our daily lives, not even into the lives of those of us who use it extensively and regularly or who write about it. Indeed, much of its early appeal, I conjecture, is that it still remains something of an exciting adventure to log-on and fly off in exploration into the wild blue cyber-yonder. Sure, it's still damned slow, the line often drops, systems crash when trying out some new feature, files get lost or do not always reach their intended destination: we cannot help but be aware of the interface that is our sometimes tenuous at best connection with the Internet.

And yet, will it ever be as exciting again as in these heady and pioneering early days? Indeed, once the web is fully integrated seamlessly into our everyday lives, will we ever be able to see and examine the whole web phenomenon as clearly as we can now?

The evolution of the graphical interface – all an elaborate illusion

If a computer does little more than translate surges of electric energy or digital impulses, it is the user interface that translates these invisible surges, these strings of binary code – no more than 'on' or 'off' switches – into a format that we can understand and relate to, indeed, lately even have meaningful relationships with. Reaching a thorough understanding of how the personal computer actually achieves this, though of a certain esoteric interest, is of no more relevance to this book than finding out how the telephone works, or unravelling the mysteries of the radio. But a basic understanding of the evolution of the personal computer user interface itself is instructive as it has had, and will continue to have, a direct impact on the formation and structure of content on the World Wide Web.

How startlingly quick this evolution has been, too, the speed of electronic change continuing at remarkable pace, in particular in comparison with the centuries that preceded our age during which the book essentially remained in its present form, the primary receptacle and purveyor of all written human knowledge. The personal computer, on the other hand, has been around for but a few decades, and during this time, literally before our very eyes, we have witnessed such a phenomenal development in both hardware – it is said that the power of an average desktop PC is far greater than that of the computer in the 1960s that in size took up a whole room or rooms – as well as in the software that drives it.

Witness, furthermore, how the personal computer has become the primary tool for content creation as well as content delivery – writing, design and layout, even the generation and supply of digital imagery and illustration. As a writer, over the course of a relatively brief career spanning just a few decades, I have myself experienced in my professional life the progressive move from pen and paper to the manual typewriter,[2] electric typewriter, electronic daisywheel typewriter, rudimentary word processor (little more than a glorified typewriter with a two line screen that allowed errors to be corrected before being printed), to, in my case, various manifestations, always ever more powerful, of the Apple Macintosh personal computer hooked up to various output devices (dot matrix printer, laserwriter, colour inkjet printer, etc.).

The development in the early 1980s of the Apple Macintosh together with its reliance on the use of the mouse was a significant breakthrough in the evolution of the personal computer user interface because it allowed digital information to be viewed, interacted with and related to primarily in a graphical form utilising a familiar visual metaphor, the desktop, that most of us, even the most computer illiterate, could quickly and intuitively relate to. The Mac desktop operating system, later emulated in essential philosophy by Microsoft with its Windows interface, was so successful that most of us today have come to take this desktop metaphor for granted (though there are, I know, still pockets of extremists, diehard MS-DOSers and command-liners lurking around out there somewhere). We accept, for example, that multiple documents can be on screen at the same time, but that the top document is the active one, just like the top piece of paper on the desk is the one which deserves or demands our immediate attention in physical space. Clicking the mouse on a document buried below brings it to the top of the pile, just as we rustle about with the bits of paper buried on our physical desks (who said the PC would result in the paperless office?). It is furthermore commonly accepted that documents are tidied away into folders, and that folders themselves are nested within other folders, to be opened with a click or double click of the everpresent and hardworking mouse.

Deep down, though we may suspect – and realise for sure when, from time to time, our systems crash – that it is all but an elaborate illusion, the digital bits of raw information not actually tidied up in physical space anywhere at all but rather cast randomly about our hard disks in unrelated bundles and packets. It is but the user interface that allows us to make mental sense of it all.

Similarly, the tools of content creation themselves make use of elaborate illusion and metaphor. The desktop publishing revolution has relied on metaphors from the world of traditional production and publishing, in part, I imagine, because it made new electronic tools more comprehensible to those more used to working in the old ways. For an elaborate multi-column layout, text and images are 'cut' and 'pasted' as if, for all the world, scissors and glue are still involved (a process that I remember well). Whether using a bitmap painting program or a vector-based drawing program, tools such as 'pencils', 'rubbers', 'spray cans' and much more allow us to create strings of digital code that result in rich and colourful digital imagery.

The intelligent web browser

The movement from the personal computer as content creation tool to the personal computer as an electronic global publishing medium is based on a similar illusion, the attempt, more or less successfully at present time, to take those strings of digital code, routed and rerouted in seemingly random packets across the open architecture network that is the Internet, then to reassemble them in a form and manner that makes more or less sense at the user's end. Indeed, when Tim Berners-Lee first conceived of what has come to be the World Wide Web, his idea was based on the principle that smart servers and smart browsers capable of understanding HTML by means of Hypertext Transfer Protocol – the 'http' of every web URL address would be able to translate intelligently the digital information that the Internet was capable of carrying and delivering.

But we have already noted that Berners-Lee's vision was of an essentially structure- not appearance-oriented web, the principle being that it would be the user's choice of interface that would interpret the digital information so delivered, and so consequently determine the display of that content. Though users would be utilising myriad combinations of hardware, operating systems, processor speed, monitor size, and a host of other hardware variables, the delivery of such digital content was to be dependent on the interface or web browser, which itself replaced other more arcane and difficult to navigate Internet protocols such as FTP, gopher, telnet and usenet (all of which are still in use, reminding us that the World Wide Web is but a small, if ever growing part, of the much larger Internet).

Indeed, it is not going too far to say that the very success and popularity of the web, allowing it to enter into mainstream life rather than remain in the corridors of academia, or scientific or military institutions, is due precisely to the development of that interface, and in particular the development of a graphic web browser that permitted the delivery of not just text, but also of images and even sound and video, the digital bits all pieced together through Berners-Lee's essentially simple HTML code and interpreted at the users' ends through the web browser rather like the construction of an intricate electronic puzzle or, more poetically, a mosaic made up of many digital bits and pieces.

What the National Center for Supercomputing Application's (NCSA) early web browser, dubbed Mosaic, did for the web is similar to what the Macintosh operating system did for the personal computer: at a stroke, it liberated users from arcane text-driven file systems to a colourful world of visual simplicity, and in the process facilitated the eventual creation of an electronic publishing medium capable of delivering true multimedia content. The implications of this development for the form and structure, indeed the very nature of content itself, should by no means be underestimated: for the development of the graphic web browser took a medium originally created for a narrow scientific community into the realms of mainstream accessibility and consequently opened up an entire new universe of content – personal, commercial, corporate, consumer, entertainment and much else.

The 'browser wars'

Since the early days of Mosaic, there has been a headlong rush to develop ever more powerful and sophisticated web browsers, a rush fueled by a corporate competition that is so fierce that it has been dubbed the 'browser wars'. Netscape Communications, the brainchild of Marc Andreessen, who at NCSA was a co-creator of Mosaic, Jim Clark, founder of Silicon Graphics, and James Barksdale, former CEO at AT & T, can be credited with the development of the commercial web browser through the creation of Netscape Navigator. Though the earliest version of Netscape was very much Mosaic-derived, it had features that were more acceptable to the general user (rather than to the academic or technically minded). The interface was more streamlined with large buttons that the user could interact with intuitively.

Subsequent versions extended the power of the web browser further. Netscape 2.0, for example, more successfully integrated its e-mail package into the browser environment, and at the same time started an unfortunate trend of introducing proprietary tags that extended HTML to support new functions not catered for by Berners-Lee's original but fairly rudimentary mark-up language.[3] Netscape 3.0 supported the use of java and javascript, while Netscape Gold incorporated not only a web browser, but a web editor, thus introducing a software package that linked the activities and tools for both accessing the web as well as creating web sites, a significant step forward. The latest available version at the time of writing (but most certainly not at the time that you read this) is Netscape Communicator 4.5, which takes this trend of converging media even further, combining a most powerful web browser, which supports the latest version of HTML 4.0 including such dynamic features as layers, cascading style sheets, java and javascript; a web editor or content creation tool in Netscape Composer; total e-mail integration; a newsreader; conferencing software and much more. Naturally the size of this heavyweight software package is considerable, as are its requirements for memory, hard disk space, and third-party plug-ins. But nonetheless, the evolution of Netscape from its rudimentary origins in the early days of the web to the sophisticated and complicated suite of applications that it has become is a further indication of how the web, and our expectations and demands of it, have similarly evolved.

So popular and successful was Netscape, and so rampant the growth of new web users in the mid-1990s, that Navigator's use increased expotentially and for a time the company had virtually cornered the web browser market, with Navigator accounting for as much as 80 to 85 per cent, with Mosaic a poor and distant second; in the process, the small high-tech company had similarly ballooned to a corporation employing some 1,800 people and generating serious revenues (in 1996) of some $346 million.

Success may, it seems, inevitably breed hubris. Andreesen and Clark, new media icons due to their fantastic and meteoric success and wealth, even began to envisage a time when the web browser itself could come to take the place of the PC operating system by making use of advanced technology such as platform-independent java and thus herald a new generation of the NC or network computer.

The merest whisper of a platform that could threaten Microsoft's domination of the operating system market via its various manifestations of Windows brought Bill Gates belatedly into the fray, but once Microsoft committed itself to the Internet, it made full use of its considerable human and financial resources. The company's subsequent development of Internet Explorer, which has gradually but inexorably clawed considerable market share away from Netscape, has been achieved both by giving it away free to new web users[4] as well, more importantly, by creating a product that is so closely integrated into the Microsoft Windows work environment as to interact virtually seamlessly within it. Such has been the success of Microsoft strategy that over a relatively brief time, it may have already reached parity with Netscape in market share, indeed by the time you read this, even exceeded it.

But has Microsoft been competing on a level playing field? The United States Department of Justice was sufficiently concerned to begin an investigation that has ultimately led to the courts. At the time of writing, the case of The United States Government, Petitioner, versus Microsoft Corporation, Respondent, is on-going and not yet resolved. There have been allegations that the company attempted to coerce computer manufacturers who pre-install Microsoft's Windows operating system software on the PCs they produce to include as a precondition the web browser Internet Explorer. In other words, by compelling PC manufacturers to include Internet Explorer on all new PCs using Microsoft's operating system, the company, it is alleged, was thus ensuring that its product could achieve market share dominance at the unfair expense of the competition.

Microsoft, on the other hand, apparently argues that Internet Explorer, far from being an extra or additional piece of software, is in fact an integrated component of its operating system and that it claims the right to be able to dictate the composition of that operating system.

The case is far from being resolved, and the browser war clearly looks set to run and run for some time to come. Make no mistake, it is a battle of more than merely passing interest for the content creator and indeed all web users. It is a battle with implications that extend far beyond merely giving the user the choice of picking this or that web browser to surf with. For whoever controls the shape and form of the browser through which most users access content on the web to a large extent may be in a position to influence and in some ways control the form and shape and direction of that very content itself (content developed for browsers for web TV may necessarily differ from content developed for browsers used on multimedia PCs, for example).

An innovative but as yet mainly unnoticed and still not fully exploited feature on Internet Explorer 4.0 hints at what could be around the next corner: channels. By adding a new and powerful layer of navigation, the web browser at the click of a button (or several) has elevated itself to the position of web content determiner and has opened the floodgates to the concept of premium brands or mega-channels driven by corporate content creators. It is by no means fanciful to envisage that Microsoft (or any other web browser supplier) could enter into deals with content providers to ensure that their browsers come preloaded with such channels up-front and to the fore. The days when the small site creator had just as much chance of succeeding as the multinational corporation may well be coming to an end: for as the web browser presents to the user no longer an unlimited and infinite choice of web sites on virtually everything under the sun, but instead a filtered and relatively limited, familiar and comfortable choice of channels offering a mix of content and no doubt heavy corporate advertising, the small sites will inevitably retreat and regroup into the realms of niche or specialist publishing.

'The battle for the living room'[5]

Meanwhile, a far larger battle is underway that may well make the Netscape/Microsoft tussle seem little more than a storm in a proverbial cup of java. For if the latest versions of both companies' browsers are indeed heavyweight and impressive packages, both undoubtedly require the muscle of the most powerful and up-to-date PCs to drive them efficiently and effectively. But is the PC truly the future way that we as users will continue to access the World Wide Web? Not if the electronic giants like Sony, Philips, Lucky Goldstar, and others have their way. Indeed, as the web moves from the office to the living room by way of web TV and the promise of interactive digital TV, and as we, together with a new demographic base of users that at present doesn't have or even want access to computers, comes of age, there will be the inevitable move towards ever greater convergence of media through a single interface. As a consequence, the future of the interface, and by definition the content that it delivers, looks set to change ever more radically.

The first generation of the web TV browser, certainly, is not anywhere near as powerful, nor does it need to be, as the desktop web browser (though by the time you read this, second, perhaps even third generation browsers will be gracing our living rooms). Some of the early browsers currently available, for example, do not fully support such standards as frames and java or javascript, features that web users have come to expect. Thus at a time when content creation is moving towards ever more sophisticated layouts and precise control of design elements by way of HTML 4.0 and XML using dynamic features such as layers and cascading style sheets, a new generation of less powerful web browsers driven by the prospect of access through the television is competing and may even come eventually to dominate the home market.

There are important implications to these dual strands of development. Will the person who accesses the web through TV necessarily be more passive and less demanding than the web user on a PC, the proverbial couch potato turned mouse potato? Indeed, is it safe to assume, as the manufacturers seem to be doing, that a lower level of technical expertise will be required by the web TV user, who, only finally having just mastered the intricacies of working the video recorder, would be resistant, for example, to going through the digital rigmarole of updating browser versions *ad infinitum,* or searching for the latest plug-ins to get innovative content to play? The major web channels that eventually emerge no doubt will cater for this market to a greater and greater degree, but will this necessarily mean a limiting of the avant-garde, the cutting edge sites that push the medium to its limit? Or will high end content that makes use of the most advanced technologies and features currently available and to come in the future continue to be developed for a more sophisticated user base that remains faithful to the desktop PC?

We have already noted the trend in web site creation which, through the creation of the Home page, looks set to continue. Homesteading or site building has emerged as a recreational activity in its own right, a pastime that complements the activity of surfing the web. Some new media analysts predict that as many as 20 to 50 percent of web users will eventually have their own web space.[6] But as the web moves from the office to the living room, is it not probable that the activities of web surfing and web creation may diverge? The web TV browsers simply won't have the necessary tools packaged within them – web editors, graphics manipulation packages, java enablers, etc – to enable effective site creation from the comfort of the sofa. Television, moreover, has historically been a passive, not a creative experience.

The spatial and environmental dimensions of web access should not be ignored either. With the PC, most of us normally sit about 18 inches away from the screen; television viewers often watch from across the room. Will the increasing use of web TV lead the web to become a less text-driven medium than it is at present? As bandwidth increases, will it in fact become more like TV only interactive? A hint of the shape of things to come is the broadcasting of episodic web programmes, that is, programmes shot like traditional television shows and broadcast exclusively over the web in episodes that aim to have the feel and look of mainstream TV broadcasts. (The existing problem of limited bandwidth has been dealt with by push technology that allows viewers to download episodes overnight, while those with cable modems or existing high speed connections can watch the show live in real time.)

But what a palaver, what an adventure just to get what TV can already deliver so effortlessly. Indeed this example does but show up the current limitations of the web as a real time broadcasting medium, as well as highlighting its relative difficulty of use compared to 'turn on the set and switch off your mind' media like TV. Compared to traditional media, the web undoubtedly is still very user unfriendly: complicated to access, and often frustratingly slow due to the continued congestion of limited bandwidth. Such problems intensify a sense of information overload due to the poor and unprofessional quality of much of the information currently available, inevitable since the web empowers everyone to be a publisher, even when they perhaps have little worthwhile to publish.

What seems certain is that our expectations as users in front of PCs are likely to be very different than our expectations as users on the sofa in the living room. Will the movement of the web from office to home bring higher expectations and in the process help drive the industry to solve some of these perennial problems?

The use of the web, moreover, is unlikely to remain confined to just the office or the home. It is likely that in years to come we shall see an ever greater provision of web access facilities in public spaces. Cybercafés, for example, add a social element to web use. Not only do they enable those who do not have private access to the web to get on-line on a pay-as-you-view basis, moreover, the best such venues provide a real, not virtual, community meeting place where you can discuss the latest happenings in cyberspace, share new and exciting web links, or just meet people, preferably over a cup of freshly brewed java. Many public libraries throughout Europe, the United States, and elsewhere offer web access as a public information resource (and raise questions about freedom of speech and censorship, a topic that we look at in a later chapter). And in Holland, public web kiosks, similar in form and concept to public telephones, have already been installed on street corners in Amsterdam and Rotterdam. These web kiosks function through the use of a normal phonecard and give access both to the web and e-mail, with a screen and keyboard that is apparently fully weatherproof.

Indeed as the facility to access the web expands beyond both the office and the living room, new considerations will need to be given to spatial and environmental aspects of interface design as well as to the ergonomics of hardware appliance design.

Towards an intelligent and adaptive interface

At present there is at once, on the one hand, a movement towards an ever more powerful and sophisticated user interface that utilises the latest technologies and 'killer applications' as Netscape and Microsoft compete relentlessly with each other and new browser versions emerge, ever larger, ever more bloated and memory hungry, with frightening frequency. On the other hand, meanwhile, web TV and other not yet invented appliances promise a less complicated web world where user friendliness is the key to the interface, but at the expense of features and ways of interacting that many of us have come to expect from new media.

Take the keyboard itself, for example. Will tomorrow's mouse potatoes wish to go through the elaborate and relatively thoughtful process (compared to pushing a button on a TV remote control) of inputting complicated URLs anymore than Mac users would wish to give up their beloved visual interface and return to using arcane command-line instructions? Indeed, will text still be the dominant means of purveying information on the web if we are seated on sofas across the room from our web TV sets rather than 18 inches away from our computer monitors?

It does not take a great leap in imagination to appreciate that the relationship between the interface and its physical environment is critical to the type of content that is so delivered. Content must inevitably be altered in shape and form as the web moves out of the relatively sterile realms of the office (consider, for example, that most office PCs do not have sound cards, not least because of the cacophony that they would bring to the office environment) into the living room. As a new generation of appliances is developed for different situations – the video telephone that allows web access and e-mail access, wearable browsers, the web browser on a microwave oven in the kitchen that can link to food and recipe sites and order groceries as you need them, a pocket web browser that you take with you when travelling: these are all products that are already in production – content will be developed to service the new and changing environments and situations in which we will access the web.

Indeed, it seems clear that that which we currently accept in the office, sometimes grudgingly, sometimes in a more generous and forgiving spirit (but let's be honest, it's easy to be generous if someone else is paying the phone bills), will not find acceptance in the living room, where attention spans are shorter, habits (the nervous, twitchy finger on the remote control) more ingrained. The drive, then, must be towards a user interface that is even easier, more intuitive than existing media, not more complicated. Could voice-operated software be one way of achieving this? The development of the voice driven intelligent agent as interface – our own personal electronic butlers, programmed to recognize not only our voices but to anticipate our own needs and desires even in advance of us knowing them ourselves – is certainly one area for future development.

And yet, the paradox remains that representing the fragmented and intricate digital universe we now inhabit is going to require a more complex visual language, not a simpler and easier one. The desktop metaphor can no longer satisfy our cyber-cravings, and indeed, even the high end web browsers currently available, by the very limitations inherent within HTML, manage to reduce content often to the lowest common denominator. We grope in vain, creating visual and structural metaphors to define and identify our electronic habitations: virtual shopping malls, virtual museums, the web site as edifice, as town square, as café or pub. Perhaps the development of virtual reality tools that will enable us to create more and more realistic 3D virtual environments that we can inhabit may be another way that tomorrow's interface will help us to navigate and travel through cyberspace.

But the danger remains that when the needs of the mouse potato become paramount, when commerce and premium brands and commercial broadcasting channel models come to the fore and are the motor that drives interface development, the web risks following the path of television in opting for the lowest or indeed most moronic common denominator. In the process, must we inevitably sacrifice something of the infinite richness, the sheer, beautiful chaos of the digital universe that we now inhabit, warts and all?

Should we not be seeking, instead, to find an interface that helps us to achieve a more thoughtful means of exploring and travelling through cyberspace rather than a less thoughtful one. The influence of computer games coupled with television culture – the ever present remote control that allows us to switch between a hundred channels without watching any of them – have in the last generation or so, made us all so very impatient, and we need to beware of this tendency. Web browsing at present is an activity that at times seems little different from the frenzy of Nintendo computer games, the activity of TV channel surfing, the switching from site to site with all the intoxicating thrills of speeding through digital cyberspace. Is it, can it ever be possible to have a thoughtful and reflective relationship with reading matter and content on the web when the interface, with its blinking colours, images, buttons that buzz or sing, urge us ever to move on, promising the same childish excitement and anticipation as when we visit the fun fair? The book, by contrast, appears positively staid and stolid in comparison, but we ignore the thoughtful, long established solidity of that form at our peril. Certainly, amidst all the euphoria and excitement, it is essential that content creators give consideration to the needs and expectations of the electronic reader.

For ultimately, interface design is not just about aesthetics, not just about the design and appearance of the computer screen or the web TV that we view. Rather it is actually about the way we live, and the way we interact, both with and between ourselves as well as with our computers and other electronic devices and appliances. I began this chapter with the assumption that the web interface is the surface forming a common boundary between ourselves and cyberspace. Does that interface itself, with its multiple layers based on links and hyperlinks that carry us out of ourselves, its encouragement for us to switch on and surf at high speed through endless pages and documents and sites, themselves all located anywhere in the world and written and produced by individuals or companies with points of view or attitudes or values that may be radically different from our own and from each other, interconnected only in the most tenuous way, in fact lead us towards a more confusing, fragmentary experience of the world? Or is it but a reflection of our own making: the world today, as we approach the millenium in a postmodern state of fragmentation, confusion, and multi-cultural, multiple viewpoints?

It is as well to remember that, just as it is essential that the modern interface should allow us seamlessly to connect to content on the web, so is it equally important that the interface integrates into our daily lives in such a way that we are still able to act and interact with each other as human beings.

1 The promise of portable hand-held devices that will be able to access on-line literature and 'books' has long been dangled before us, and prototypes should be on the market by the time you read this. From the early examples that I have seen and read about, few would appear to be serious rivals to the book, though I may well be proved wrong on this.

2 It is an indication of how quickly this evolution has taken place that my children – and many others – have never actually seen a typewriter, that now antique tool of content creation that in the developed world at least has been virtually consigned to the dustbin of history.

3 The trend of competing proprietary extensions, sometimes even requiring proprietary plug-ins, has led to the sometimes ridiculous situation where web developers and designers have had to create sites for particular browsers, knowing that they would look considerably different on competing browsers. This situation is not yet resolved and indeed looks set to continue.

4 Netscape, realising the importance of keeping market share, announced in early 1998 that it would cease from selling the Netscape Navigator suite of web browsers and in the future give it away free, as well as the code to third party developers, thus at a stroke enlisting an army of unpaid software developers and users to assist in its further testing. A potentially more significant development is the merging of November, 1998 of Netscape and AOL thus bringing together web browser, AOL's proprietary content, and millions of subscribers.

5 The title for this sub-section comes from the title of a compelling and fascinating set of lectures given by James Woodhuysen, Prof of Innovations, DeMontfort University, to the University of Plymouth, Feb 1997 and the 'Crosscurrents'conference at the Phoenix Arts Centre, Exeter, March 1999. Woodhuysen is always thought provoking and challenging in his views about the future of new media and its potential impact on our lives.

6 'How the Web was Won', *Guardian On-line* 19 March 1998 p. 2

CHAPTER FOUR

The Medium, the Message, and Content

By the early years of the 21st century, a generation will have grown up with digital media an integral part of their lives. This is bound to have – and is already having – a profound impact on the way they will think, learn, work, play, shop, make love, in short perceive the world, just as a generation ago, television brought with it a new and profound shift in the way of viewing and perceiving our surroundings that we all now take for granted, a technicolour vision of a world shrunk ever smaller, less abstract, more vibrant if fragmented and multicultural than the previous solid resonance of the aural world of radio, and the reassuringly rhythmic black-and-white typographical patterns that preceded it. Indeed, we may soon if not already have reached that moment of critical mass when the web ceases anymore to be 'new technology' but rather embodies and represents a genuine, profound, and probably irreversible cultural shift that effects us all.

Certainly the generation that will grow up taking new digital media completely for granted, that is, the privileged generation that will have access to it, will be able to grasp, benefit from, enjoy and exploit the new digital media in ways not yet even imagined. In fact, however, a real opportunity lies before all of us at this fortunate moment in time to open our minds to the possibilities that the digital cyberworld presents to us. But just as it is important to state this belief (not least because so many still have a fear and a reluctance to embrace digital media), so is it also important to attempt to define and understand how cyberculture and the web are impacting on our daily lives. Indeed, this is the challenge of understanding digital media: if the medium is the message, then how will the web extend our perceptions, our experiences, our expression and self-expression of what it is to be alive on Earth at the turn of the second millenium?

Net culture and the empowerment of the user

It does not seem to be possible to write about the web without attempting therefore to gain an understanding about some of the emerging elements that collectively make up what could be called 'net culture'. To do so of course is to risk ridicule, for the act is something akin to that in the fable of the blind men attempting to describe an elephant by that part of anatomy which each is able to feel. The whole remains amorphous, beyond view, ever changing, growing and evolving: we can but see a part, never the whole.

What seems certain already is that this profound cultural shift that net culture represents is going to have an ever more important impact on our lives, giving new tonal values to those sets of assumptions that we may previously have held unquestioningly about the world and our place in it. Perhaps this shift is but a manifestation of larger and broader symptoms, our postmodern, post-Cold War condition at the end of a millenium, living in a multicultural world that is ever more fragmented, more complex, with fewer straightforward answers to fundamentally deep and mysterious questions.

The concept of non-linear hypertext, for example, represents a profound shift from the more stable way that content has been viewed for the past several centuries. Hypertext is not just about adding electronic annotations to static, flat text; rather, it represents a radical shift in thought patterns and means of presenting information that can be explored at random or in any order, in as great or as shallow depth as required, reordered and even recreated by the user. Entered or exited by multiple doors and given depth and extra dimension through hyperlinks both that lead elsewhere as well as those that bring users to the text or document from unknown or remote locations, non-linear hypertext is by definition multi-layered, rather like an onion skin, sometimes opaque, but usually at the least semi-transparent in the relationships that it creates. It is this semi-transparent quality that is perhaps most appealing, granting users greater power and control over where they wish to go. But at the same time, content is no longer certain as to its ultimate destination.

The web has also turned on its head traditional roles of active content creator or author and passive reader or viewer, for it contains within its workings the built-in assumption that content is interactive. Web users are not content to sit back, like the previous generation of couch potatoes in front of the TV, and passively absorb whatever is offered to them; they want to, expect to, need to be actively involved with it, searching for what they want, going off on tangential journeys, interacting with the content creator, writing or adding their own comments or opinions.

This means too that content is no longer accepted at face value; rather, it is constantly questioned, commented upon, even altered or rejected. The fluid nature of web content is normally able to accomodate such interactivity and indeed able to benefit from such vigorous interactive dialogue. In this respect, the user has the potential to enter into something of a unique partnership with the content creator; indeed in some cases the users even become the constructors and content creators themselves.

This implies a completely different potential model of content creation. Rather than a site being constructed by the author from the top down, like some great elaborate edifice, flying buttresses and all, a web site can often be published on the fly in a still evolving state that has the capacity to grow organically, nurtured and cared for by both content creator and the users who access it and give interactive encouragement and the actual contribution of new material.

Inherent is the view that content is not something that is either carved in stone or even set in anything so permanent as moveable type. Rather, like flickering patterns of light on the screen, it is shockingly ephemeral: the page you visit today may very well not be there in its same state tomorrow. For if content is not static then it must be active, something that needs to be constantly generated and regenerated through creativity, innovation and an ever-surging and renewable energy. The web page that does not change is a static and dead page.

Another alteration in our perceptions which the web has brought about is that space and distance, in miles and in cultures, may have very little meaning. The metaphor of the world as a global village is indeed a potent one that net culture positively fosters. Net culture has truly and effortlessly done more to break down national and linguistic frontiers than even such grand political organisations as the European Union or The United Nations and the world is a smaller and arguably better place for it. But is this sense of community engendered in part because of the still exciting newness of the web, a feeling of belonging to a secret and privileged club, with its own language, its secret funny handshake? When everyone is on-line, or at least the predicted 200-odd million or so by the turn of the millenium, will this cosy *ménage* have disappeared, with people feeling nothing more in common with other fellow web users than with those who also own a telephone or a TV?

Arm-in-arm with the diminuation of space and distance that the web brings, there has also been a notable movement towards greater global convergence and this is accelerating at an ever faster rate. On-line activity undoubtedly alters the way we live and work and while it at once brings the world closer together, it is sometimes at the expense of multicultural identity and diversity, especially since English has established itself as the *lingua franca* of the web. This movement towards greater and greater cultural convergence is certainly something to be aware, indeed beware, of.

In today's era of electronic media, the message is that the web, and the whole net culture which it represents and which is represented through it, has undoubtedly and probably permanently altered the way we interact with content and indeed even with each other.

Creativity and technology

Of course McLuhan's famous aphorism 'the medium is the message' implies that the technology itself is the ultimate determinant of content and more. What is most interesting in the case of the World Wide Web is to consider how technological innovation is impacting on creativity and in the process resulting in a form that is evolving organically in unpredictable directions. Indeed this is a medium that is positively driven by technological innovation, and as new so-called 'killer applications' arrive on the scene in ever greater and more frequent profusion, it is possible to witness the evolution of the form most graphically. Witness how static and unimaginative early first generation web sites now seem, with their grey backgrounds, and lists of hypertext links extending down the screen in sometimes endless scrolls. Yet how exciting they appeared to us just, what, a few years ago? As new features have come on line, both as extensions to HTML as well as through plug-in technologies, web sites have literally come alive, with the imaginative use of graphics, frames, and tables used not simply to liven up a page but to aid in navigation and the facility of exploration.

Macromedia's Shockwave[1] plug-in, for example, allows the importation of Director movies, Flash animations and streaming audio and video.[2] This facility adds true multimedia capabilities to the web, and with the use of Macromedia's lingo script, dynamic interactivity is possible whereby, for example, certain behaviours – the start of a sound file, the swapping of an image, or the offer of a pull-down menu – take place when a mouse rolls over an image or is clicked on. However, such features come at a cost, and that is the requirement for the user to have the Shockwave plug-in installed and configured in his browser as an in-line helper application. Though this is freely available from the Macromedia site, to download the application can be at once time consuming and off-putting even to advanced web users.

Shockwave is not the only technology that requires a third-party plug-in. Checking my web browser at this moment, I discover that I have no fewer than 12 third-party helper applications configured and this number grows literally almost by the day, virtually every time I come across an interesting or innovative site that requires some widget application to get it to work. Some of the more common innovative technologies that require third party plug-ins in order to make such files accessible include streaming audio and video, VRML (virtual reality markup language provides a means by which 3D environments can be described and interpreted for representation and navigation within a web browser), Adobe Acrobat (for the delivery and accessing of design-rich PDF portable document format files), Flash Shockwave (for vector animations), and many others.

The result is that the web is becoming ever more fragmented with such a plethora of proprietary plug-in extensions in use and few as yet establishing themselves as true industry standards that it has become difficult for the content creator to know which to choose, safe in the knowledge that a site will be able to be at once at the cutting edge yet at the same time be able to reach a large audience. Technology in this sense is causing the web to grow ever more tangled and confusing, the haves and have-nots no longer merely delimited by those who are or are not on-line, but further by those who utilise the latest browser versions or who are savvy enough to have downloaded and configured the requisite 'cutting edge' helper applications necessary to make cool sites really sing and dance. The frustration for those who come across such sites but find themselves shut out from their full features can be extreme and lead to the situation where users feel compelled constantly to keep up with the latest applications or risk being consigned to the dustbin of net oblivion.

Java[3] and the simpler though closely related javascript are two object-oriented, cross-platform computer languages that hold considerable promise as alternative means to adding interactivity and functionality that can be delivered without the need for third-party plug-ins within a java-savvy web browser.[4] Javascript programs, written as lines of code within an HTML page, for example, can control the behaviour of a page, helping to determine not only how it looks, but how it acts and interacts with the user. At its most basic level, javascripts are used primarily for ornamentation – scrolling text, buttons that change colour when triggered by events such as a mouse rollover or click, the playing of a background sound file. Java applets have the potential to be more powerful and can be used to create substantive cross-platform applications that one day may even take care of all the tasks your computer currently does, working off networked terminals that download software applications on demand.

However, though java and javascript programs do not require plug-ins to run, it is not all plain sailing: at present both devour valuable bandwidth to operate and so can slow down sites considerably. Content creators utilising java or javascript in web development must therefore balance the time it takes to wait for an applet to download or a script to execute against the perceived value of that application.[5] More worryingly, these so-called 'universal cross-platform languages' are beginning to appear in various platform-, appliance-specific, or proprietary guises and versions. So as in everything else on the web, the promise of universal accessibility is easier than the delivery.

The whole thing at times rather reminds me of those hi-fi fanatics from the 1970s and 80s, you know, those folks who were insanely 'into' stereo components – amps, pre-amps, the latest turntables,[6] speakers with massive subwoofers and the clearest and most precise tweeters – but were hardly interested at all in the music that they could enjoy through the machine. It was the sheer excitement of those sexy objects of desire that was the driving force behind their enthusiasms. I see the same thing sometimes in the web whiz kids today who can't wait to cram their sites with the latest electronic equivalents for the sheer sake of it, the technology an end in itself rather than a means to communicating or adding value to content. I see it too in myself, in other web users who feel that it is essential to keep up with all that is the latest. This too is the meaning of the 'medium is the message'.

Technology, it seems certain, is going to continue to drive the web for the near future and in the process lead us ever more into temptation. Like electronic junkies, it is hard not to get addicted to the thrill of it all. This is indeed a great part of the excitement of developing creative content for the web. Undoubtedly, the entire creative process is undergoing an extended period of trial and error and the learning curve is still steep, the mistakes and blunders egregious. Those technologies that are truly worthwhile, meanwhile, will ultimately, and hopefully sooner rather than later, establish themselves as industry standards simply through passing that point of critical mass wherein such a large number utilise a technology that it becomes no longer an option but a necessity.

So it is not only a question of discovering what new technologies are effective, it is also a case of finding out what users will go for. Indeed, the finest or funkiest special effect or application may bring orgasmic joy and satisfaction to the content creator but, for any variety of reasons – slow download, the requirement of a third-party plug-in, for example – prove to be a total turn-off, or click-elsewhere for the user (and the advent of web TV and the mouse potato mentality that this may further engender is only likely to bring greater resistance to such requirements). Finding the balance between those new technologies that are of real worth and interest yet which are capable of reaching as large an audience as possible will not always be easy.

Content as community
Of course, reaching a mass audience is not necessarily always the be-all and end-all of web publishing. Perhaps the most interesting and recurring concept that has emerged as an element of net culture is that of content as community, the way that electronic media truly is capable of bringing people together, yes, in large massed groups[7] as well as in tiny, niche communities made up of individuals who share even the most obscure special interests or activities. This concept of content as community puts web publishing and web content creation

within an important social and contextual framework that says much about our needs as individuals in an age of uncertainty and alienation.

What is it about the web that compels us, each alone (usually) in front of our PC or web TV, to come into communication, even communion with others of similar interests, themselves similarly facing the flickering screens of their PCs remotely located anywhere else in the world? As in the real world, it seems, people are attracted like moths to an electronic candle by the universal yearning to be part of a larger group that shares common values and interests. Thus, virtual communities, like real world communities, become at once places where people can meet, connect with one another, share interests, argue vociferously, make love (virtually), sell and buy goods from one another, play games, and much else. Indeed, the very nature of web content, its inherent interactivity, has built into it the propensity to create communities, for when users who access information or a site can interact with both the site creator or with other users of that same site, then the process has begun.

Chat rooms are one of the most important means of building communities on the web, for they provide the possibility of meeting and interacting with individuals or groups of individuals directly and in real time (as opposed to asynchronous communication through, say, e-mail discussion groups). The chat room implies an intimate and enclosed space where we are safe to confide and converse with whomsoever we should happen to meet or encounter there. Of course when we enter such an electronic space, we know that we are not all in the same room physically; rather by taking part in the sharing of minds and thoughts over shared networks there is a sense of the creation of some metaphysical cyberspace which we collectively share during our time spent there. In chat rooms we make 'cyberfriends' and 'cyberbuddies'. We can make 'buddy lists' so that we know who and when others are live on-line, and we can even indulge in 'cybersex' ('how was it for you, dear, did the computer move?').

This is all very exciting. But the question needs to be asked: how real, how truly satisfying are such electronic community spaces for those who frequent them? My own experience is that they often leave quite a lot unsaid, quite a lot still to be desired and answered. Thus, it seems probable that as the web evolves, users are going to demand more and more from their on-line communities and virtual environments. The visual complexity of such environments where people meet may lead to an ever greater use, for example, of VRML for the construction of 3D models that have the capacity to give a spatial dimension to the flat screen, allowing individuals and groups to interact with each other not only in real time but within the rules and limitations of a spatial virtual world, moving in and out of rooms, for example, bumping into each other, or interacting with objects as well as people. And just as the environments themselves evolve, so will our representations of on-line personae in the shape of avatars – the 3D models that come to represent the user, taking on different characters and personalities through appearance, actions and dress, and through which the virtual environment is explored. The prospect of such virtual reality worlds, peopled by our other selves, is promising and takes the meaning of 'content as community' to literally new levels.[8]

In virtual communities, it seems that much of the excitement lies as much in what remains hidden as in what is revealed. In chat rooms, for example, people adopt unique monickers or nicknames through which they project a personality or persona that may have little bearing with their identity in real life. Gender switching, apparently, is popular, and people routinely lie about their age, activities and prowess. Is there something about the nature of the web, and social interaction that takes place across electronic networks, that positively encourages us to recreate ourselves? And does this mean that web content is inherently more unreliable than other forms?

It seems prudent, amidst the euphoric cacophony of the web evangelists, to voice real worries about the reliance on the web as community. As more people's lives become immersed in the web to the point of total submersion, there will be real human costs. The attraction and value of such communities can be very real indeed, but there is a danger that those with low self-esteem or social problems and inadequacies may retreat from the real world into the relative safety of cyberspace. There is a further danger of Internet addiction as people become ever more dependent on virtual communities to fill a void in lives lacking any sense of real community. And the lines where virtual community cross over into real community can be sometimes blurred and dangerous: there have been cases recently of sexual assaults and stalking following real meetings between individuals who made contact first in web chat rooms.

The moral? Web content has the in-built capacity to bring people together and the resultant web communities can be as interesting, as dangerous, as exciting, as kooky and kinky as any that exist in the real world. But we cannot, should not, depend on them to replace or be a substitute for real human contact any more than cybersex can or should ever be an adequate replacement or substitute for real sex.

Language and the web

The problem with web communities, I fear, may in part lie with the limitations of written language on the computer as a means of meaningful and deep communication between individuals as opposed to more directly physical social intercourse. Indeed, typed text accessed on-screen lacks at once the subtleties of face-to-face communication, the tonal and emotional nuances of the human voice over the telephone, even the idiosyncratic quirks of the handwritten letter. Such limitations are graphically demonstrated by the creation and reliance on the rather puerile and one-dimensional so-called 'emoticons' or 'cyber smileys', cute typographical ideograms that are widely used to express 'feeling' over the web either in e-mail messages or in real time chat rooms. Here are a few basic examples to give you the idea (if you don't get them, then hold the book at 90 degrees):

:-)	smiling
:-(	sad
:-@	screaming or swearing
:.-(	crying
;-)	winking
&:(	bad hair day

It is as if, frustrated by the limitations of the typed word on the screen, users are trying to eke out greater expression and feeling from the dumb and unfeeling keyboard and at the same time to communicate in a private shorthand of symbols and acronyms known and comprehensible only to a select and secret club, rather in the way that those who post ads on the personal pages of newspapers have devised their own language of acronyms that make no sense whatsoever to any but those who read such personal ads.[9] The results are hardly conducive to the expression of high feeling, and indeed can be little more than an iconic representation of the anodyne 'have a nice day'.

Yet in a world that has increasingly turned to the telephone at the expense of the written letter (partly due to satisfaction gained from immediate synchronous communication as opposed to delayed asynchronous), e-mail (and its affiliate forms such as group e-mail, newsgroup discussion lists, and electronic bulletin boards) has marked the return to written communication as a dominant form of social intercourse between individuals and groups. The significance of this should not be underestimated. Indeed, since today's university students throughout America, Europe and much of the world are given e-mail addresses as a matter of course and in their years as students grow used to relying on this

63

medium for staying in touch with friends and family, it is certain that in the process this is creating, indeed has already created, a base of informed and educated users who will continue to use this written medium for communicating in both their personal and professional lives.

What is perhaps most interesting about the phenomenon of e-mail is that the medium itself has resulted in a new form of content. E-mail messages are really quite unlike any other written form of communication, in part because of their immediacy: senders know or believe that their messages will arrive on the desk of the recipient either virtually immediately or else within minutes or hours of sending them. Thus, such messages can be at once a cross between informal memo and stream-of-consciousness ramble; letters by contrast, because they are commited to pen and paper, are usually more formal and considered, often sometimes more literary, less dashed off than most e-mail missives. An e-mail can simply be a single line, a question or a comment. Or it can be a long, rambling musing. How strange, too, that many people who have lost the habit of writing letters have now embraced writing e-mails with considerable enthusiasm. Part of the reason why this is so is the sheer ease of doing so: to reply to a received e-mail, one simply hits the Reply button (or enters an e-mail address), composes the message, and hits a Send button to despatch it to its destination, and all for free (or the cost of a local phone call). By contrast, a letter needs to be handwritten or wordprocessed, printed, then put into an envelope, taken to the post office, stamped, and physically placed in the mail slot; the recipient, meanwhile, must wait some days to receive it.

There seems as well to be something about the medium of e-mail that allows people to converse more freely than in other forms. Indeed, the immediacy, the openness of e-mail is one of its most universally appealing features. It is truly remarkable how people in all walks of life seem to be willing to share parts of themselves with total strangers utilising this new communications forum. In my own experience, I have made a number of friends simply through e-mail communication whom I have never yet met in real life, and I have furthermore been amazed at how accessible celebrities, politicians, famous writers, and ordinary people are by e-mail: it is far easier to track down someone's e-mail address then it is to find out their postal address or telephone number.

On the other hand, if the medium of e-mail has fostered a return to written communication, it has also undoubtedly given rise to a new form of writing that sometimes leaves much to be desired. An earlier medium, the telegraph, which in its time was costly due to the fact that messages were charged by the word, resulted in a clipped, sometimes cryptic shorthand style of writing known as telegraphese in order to keep missives brief. There is no excuse of cost constraints to explain the rise of similarly clipped, often sloppy, poorly constructed writing riddled with grammatical and spelling errors that characterises much e-mail communication today. People, in many cases intelligent, literate people who would otherwise never let such sloppy missives see the light of day in the form of a letter, appear quite happy to dash off routinely such error-ridden notes which they then simply dispatch at the press of a Send button without, apparently, so much as proofing or re-reading them, let alone running a spell checker, or even bothering to check for lower and upper case. And not only does the form and format of such e-missives leave much to be desired, it should furthermore be acknowledged that the content of such messages is often equally lacking in substance, the slap-dash nature of the medium an encouragement, it seems, to slap-dash and careless thought.

The e-mail essay, electronically composed then sent to any number of recipients at the click of a button, is another example of a new form of content that embodies both the advantages and disadvantages of the new medium. New writing on any subject – frivolous, travel, political, thoughtful, domestic – is facilitated, and it is possible to reach an audience that one would otherwise not be able to. Few of us, for example, have written essays, then photocopied and distributed them by post; or if we did, then it was a considerable effort, not to say expense, to do so. The e-mail essay makes such dissemination of writings easy to achieve, and thus provides writers with an audience. The danger, though, as with e-mail letters, is that the medium positively encourages sloppy, unpolished, even incomplete writing. Says Ian Frazier, editor of *The Best American Essays 1997*, 'E-mail, by the way, makes for the sloppiest essays, the speed of the technology catching nascent thoughts before they're real thoughts at all.'[10]

If e-mail communication, by letter or communal essay, embodies the informal, easy and casual nature of language on the Internet, this has furthermore been carried over onto web sites themselves. Again, as with e-mail displacing the telephone as a major means of daily and frequent communication for many, so has the web site marked a movement away from the visual arena of television back to the written word, albeit accessed through a monitor, not a piece of paper. Yet how does the medium itself have an effect on that written word? Just as language used by tabloid newspapers differs considerably from the language of the broadsheet, the physical form dictating to a certain extent both content and the representation of content, so does the web impose its own parameters on language and content.

Some centuries previously, typography and the printed word changed not only how people wrote, but also how they spoke and thought. Intelligent, literate discourse became removed from the everyday language of the people, and in the process some of the richness of slang and popular culture was inevitably lost. The web, though a medium essentially for written discourse, presents a return to a more direct and vigorous use of popular language.

At present, in web publishing everything is new, everything is young, everything is an adventure, and this dictates that an energetic and vigorous, sometimes breezy, groovy style of language is being used widely on the web. This reflects of course the fact that many web content creators are young, and the language used is the language of their generation. But fundamentally the nature of the medium itself is dictating new forms of language. This lies in part with the act of reading text on-screen, which, due to physical constraints dictates text that is neither too dense nor too challenging verbally or contextually. Put quite simply, great blocks or chunks of text are eye-fatiguing. The considered and thoughtful attention that more challenging text may demand is hard to give; just as it is more difficult to read a broadsheet newspaper on a moving underground train than the smaller and more manageable tabloid. It is not only the physical form of each but the content itself – the headlines, the style of writing, vocabulary and syntax, as well as typography and layout – that enagages the reader more or less demandingly. When one considers the time element that exists when accessing and reading web pages – for those of us who pay local telephone rates, the incessant tyranny of the metre ticking away, the phone bill mounting – it is not surprising that the web text that is most accessible is that which can be quickly scanned before clicking to another page.

As the web evolves, will we see an evolution of language and indeed will a more mature and considered way of accessing such content similarly emerge? It will certainly be interesting to chart this, but my fear is that the movement will be inevitably towards a lower common denominator resulting in, on the whole, less challenging text, with a greater reliance on visual and multimedia effects. This is bound to happen, furthermore, when web TV becomes a dominant force for web publishing, not least quite simply because TV viewers will physically sit further from their sets than the computer users of today. Does this mean that as the medium establishes itself in the mainstream, that writers' skills at creating well-crafted and complex sentences and texts may atrophy and wither away, just as the introduction of previous 'new technologies' caused other skills to be lost (the centuries old art of hand illustrating and copying illuminated manuscripts, for example, which was lost with the advent of moveable type and the printing press).

If the web is shaping the way we use the written language just as e-mail has altered the way we communicate directly with each other, it is interesting to note further how the English language has become the *lingua franca* of the web and in the process aided an ever-hastening global convergence. This has come about in great part because the countries where the web is most widely used are English speaking or have a large part of the population that has a good knowledge of English as a first or second language. But part of the great promise of the web is the ease that any individual or organisation can publish, in English or in any other language, including ideographic writing systems. As more and more local and localised content comes on-line, therefore, this current imbalance of English and especially American/English content will almost certainly be redressed.

The Home page: a revolution in self-expression and local expression

On the one hand, the web is hastening global convergence and in the process having the effect of making us all speak something approaching the same language, a process that will be accelerated if mainstream broadcasters and corporate content providers have their way and encourage passive mouse potatoes on web TV to access content through channels that are preset on browsers. But web users, it seems, may well be set to resist such impositions, and it seems likely that the medium will continue to encourage the creation of both local and niche content for small, sometimes tiny and specialised audiences. Indeed this very facility for specialised publishing to limited audiences means that the web remains at the forefront of a virtual revolution in self-expression and local expression. The rise of the Home page, that is a personal web site created by and for the individual, is clearly evidence of this. There are already well over a million Home pages created by individuals, and some experts predict that in years to come there will be upwards of 50 million Home pages on the World Wide Web.

The question needs to be asked, Why? Why are so many ordinary individuals, the majority of whom never have, presumably up to this point in their lives, written about nor presented themselves in any public or published forum, so eager and anxious now to do so on the World Wide Web? I can only imagine the reason, like Everest, is 'because it's there'. Because, quite simply, it has become possible to do so, just as the advent of moveable type made it possible for vernacular and popular literature to be created. The medium itself has become an extension of our very selves and we have been changed in the process.

Indeed, we probably need look no further for the *raison d'être* of the rise of the Home page than the fundamental human desire to leave a mark, somewhere, anywhere, to be noticed, indeed to be an individual, not, in this age of alienation, a faceless number, an employee, a nobody. Home pages are fascinating to visit, provide even something of a voyeuristic insight into the lives of ordinary people who you may know or may never meet.[11] It is remarkable how very revealing they can be (though there are obvious dangers in this) about personal, professional and family life and interests.

One of the most famous (or infamous) depending on your point of view Home pages which epitomises the desire to be seen is the Jennicam[12] site where a young woman called Jenni has installed a computer-top video camera in her bedroom which webcasts live at bi-weekly intervals using RealVideo technology. The site purports to show said young woman sleeping, writing, sitting, lying, dressing, putting on make-up, cooking, who knows what else. The site, apparently, attracts some 500,000 hits a day, an indication certainly of how many sad, lonely weirdos there are currently on-line. But those hoping to get a peek of the steamy action are likely to be disappointed. Jenni's archive footage includes clips entitled 'Jenni shows off her bathroom', 'Jenni makes hummus', 'What did Jenni get for Christmas?'. This is the personal Home page taken to its most egotistical extreme.

Jenni's mundane antics are but a reflection of the human condition in our time, the obsessive and narcissistic belief that everyone else is interested in how we look, what we do, what our interests are (and in her case, given the number of hits the site receives, they probably are). This same basic human impulse can indeed be the spur to generate much positive and valuable content. Thousands of Home pages have become forums for individuals to share information about their own personal lives and enthusiasms, hobbies, or passions. Many such sites become the authoritative sources of much informed expertise and usefully compiled information that would not be available elsewhere.

The web journal or e-diary is emerging as an art form in its own right. There are hundreds, perhaps even thousands of on-line budding Samuel Pepys, chronicling their own daily lives, sometimes loves and tribulations on a regular basis, and for all the world to read (though many publish disclaimers such as 'If you know me in person, please go away').

The web site Often[13] is a self-proclaimed 'web ring' of links to diaries that have daily or nearly daily updates, a serendipitous and seemingly random collection of on-line journals whose header entries give an insight into why people do this: 'i feel this need to proclaim who i am. this is where i do it'[14] and 'A thirty-something mother of four looks at her life past and present and tries to hear herself think over the incessant babble of inner voices'.[15] There are scores of others of this ilk that invite us to enter through their door and visit awhile; perusing them from the comfortable leisure of our own homes or offices gives one a strange sense of peeking beyond the clothed veneer of a total stranger into the raw, naked recesses of their other, secret and real selves.

Above all, the web, in allowing any individual, famous or otherwise, to create their own Home page grants all of us the chance to have a voice, and a voice that can be heard loud and clear around the world, even in once impenetrable corridors of power and influence and above the din and cacophony of the popular press. The medium empowers and extends our very being, our capacity to define and express who and where we are.

It is a power that extends even, who knows, beyond the grave. Home pages are currently being created in memory of loved ones who have departed, a most poignant electronic monument, and a means of collecting in cyberspace memories, memorabilia, writings, photographs, even voices for friends, loved ones, family, even future generations yet unborn to access.[16] Am I strange to find something weirdly comforting at this prospect?

Trust, authority, the message and the messenger

The web has empowered individuals to become publishers and indeed to write about anything under the sun or stars that interests, concerns or obsesses them. Web pages can provide a forum for personal expression against the wrongs and injustices of the world. Cyberprotest has become a legitimate means of expressing gripes against the injustice of systems, employers, organisations, and governments. Underground political groups have demonstrated the power of the medium, publishing communiqués direct on their own web sites, as well as infiltrating their opponents' web sites sometimes to quite devastating effect. Sympathisers of movements no longer need follow intermediated content published by traditional and possibly biased media to know what is going on. Events in the past year in Chiapas, China, Indonesia and most recently Kosovo have demonstrated the effectiveness of the medium as a tool for both peaceful protest and more direct action and revolution.

This means, however, that individuals with private gripes or grudges, against other individuals, corporations or governments can use the medium to create sites that reflect their own views and attitudes or to promote a private or public vendetta that may be dangerous or unreliable. Indeed there is the danger that the medium can be abused to make unfair, unwarranted, or unproven attacks or slurs on the character and moral probity of individuals and companies by their enemies. This raises serious questions of trust, authority, the message and the reliability of the messenger.

Indeed if the web is the most democratic of publishing media, it is also as a consequence probably the most unreliable. One of its great benefits is that it allows anyone to be a self-proclaimed journalist and to publish first-hand accounts of events as they happen anywhere in the world. Yet useful and immediate as such untrained observations can be, nonetheless such reports often lack the veracity and objectivity of reports from professional journalists and reporters who are on the spot. For indeed, the art of news reporting is not simply about giving first-hand observations but also about interpreting events within wider global perspectives through thoughtful and intelligent analysis.

Previous traditional media were able to control the flow of information, not least because of the effort and expense required to publish or disseminate such information: the man-hours involved in carving a stone tablet, hand copying an illuminated manuscript, setting type and printing a book, or filming a documentary. Such expense and effort granted authority to that content which did eventually emerge. But now that it has become so easy and so inexpensive to publish on the web, we may well have reason to doubt the validity of much content, uncertain of its authority, reliability, and responsibility.

The control of information on the Internet is as yet in its infancy and there are those who wish to see no control whatsoever over content published on the web. Moreover, the medium itself, we have already suggested, seems almost to encourage the recreation of ourselves, and is thus often used to deceive. But if we cannot trust the individuals we meet in chat rooms, then how can we trust companies or publishers or governments or anyone else purporting to offer fair, authoritative and honest content? Moreover, now that anyone can be a publisher, how do we distinguish and choose between that which is worth reading and the cyberbogus?

Faced with such prospects, content providers may be compelled to find creative solutions to gaining authority. The broadcast model using channels aims to grant authority by the branding of content through big-budget producers that the viewer has come to trust (rightly or wrongly but most usually complacently). Established names, both from traditional as well as new media, will come to gain our trust in this way. Similarly, paying for content is another way that value and authority can be bestowed: if the content is worthwhile enough to warrant paying for it, then it must be good, goes the reasoning. Academics, meanwhile, who now find that they can post their research and papers on university web sites will still, we imagine, seek to post articles foremost in those web sites that follow the same or similar procedures set down for paper publication, for example, refereed journals or e-journals.

The use of intelligent agents and information filters – robot agents that somehow sift through all the available information on a subject and separate the genuine and worthwhile from the faux, the ersatz – will probably be further refined in coming years, quite simply because we will all, as individuals, need some sort of computerised aids to keep the flow of information at bay. But who programs the cyberbutler for us, inputting values and moral or practical judgements?

The number of web sites is ever increasing at an exponential rate and in the process our need for assistance in such matters, for help in distinguishing the worthwhile and authoritative content that we can trust from the dross, will only increase. It is just as well, then, amidst celebrations at how the web empowers us as individuals to be publishers, to remember above all that this medium is essentially an untrustworthy one and to question just about anything we come across on it.

The web as a way of life

As the web insinuates its way into more and more aspects of our daily lives, there will reach a point when it is no longer considered new or cutting edge technology but rather merely something that is there, like the telephone or the television, a tool that we use with hardly a second thought or glance.

But the web promises further, the capacity not just to become part of our lives but, dare I say, even to represent a way of life. The richness of content that is being developed on the web, and which will continue to emerge as the medium itself evolves, suggests ways and means as to how the web is impacting on the way we live, work and play in a world that is ever more interconnected. Personal content on the web becomes an extension of our very being, we project information, enthusiasms, even personae and identities that may or may not exist in reality but which are certainly very vivid within the confines and realms of the web. Our capacities to communicate, to create, to make communities of interest and enthusiasms, to express ourselves, even to recreate ourselves, have been increased considerably by the web. Certainly there are still grave worries and reservations about the reliability of content on the web, and indeed about much of the form of that content itself (the proliferation of pornography is a real cause for concern). And yet, the breathtaking speed and ease that we have embraced it would seem to suggest that if the medium is indeed the message, like music the food of love, then what we are saying is 'play on'.

1 For more information about the Macromedia suite of web-savvy products, including Director 6.0, Dreamweaver, and Flash, visit the web site:
http://www.macromedia.com
2 Streaming audio or video means that the sound or video clips play as they are downloaded rather than having to be download entirely before playing. A player plug-

in is usually required for this to work. For further information, RealAudio is one of the leaders in the field of streaming technologies: http://www.realaudio.com

3 Some excellent resources for java and javascript are Sun's java site, 'the centre of the Java universe': http://java.sun.com; the java homepage: http://www.javasoft.com; Gamelan, a java resource and repository of much useful information about java, its development and implementation: http://www.gamelan.com; HotWired 's java page: http://www.hotwired.com/java

4 At the time of writing, Netscape 3.0 and 4.0 and IE3 and 4 support java and javascript.

5 This same caveat, of course, applies to any other features that require lengthy downloads or the retrieval of a third-party plug-in. It is no good asking people to wait some several minutes or more to download some cute widget that does nothing in terms of adding value to content and which is itself over in less than five seconds!

6 My children, who have never seen a typewriter, have rarely seen a turntable in use and are equally baffled by the stacks of vinyl records that we still have but rarely play.

7 See The Globe web site for an example of a large web site that is made up of a number of virtual communities: http://www.theglobe.com

8 A web site that allows the creation of such 3D virtual environments and communities is The Palace. A special browser as well as creation software needs to be utilised to access or create such communities and the avatars available at present are rudimentary, but the site gives a taste of what is to come: http://www.thepalace.com

9 A few web acronyms widely in use and especially prevalent in newsgroups, e-mail discussion and chat forums include: tytt (tell you the truth), rl (real life), tptb (the powers that be), tmot (trust me on this), tia (thanks in advance), btw (by the way), imho (in my humble opinion), lol (laughing out loud), rofl (roll on the floor laughing), gal (get a life).

10 Ian Frazier, editor, 1997, *The Best American Essays 1997*, Houghton Mifflin, Boston, p. xviii

11 To gain an insight into what is on offer, try, at random, visiting the personal home pages that are on sight directories like Yahoo!, service providers like AOL, or communities such as The Globe or Geocities.

12 Jennicam: http:///www.jennicam.org

13 Often: http://www.ounce.com/often/. Another web site dedicated to on-line journals is Metajournals: http://www.metajournals.com/

14 Notes from your pal Shelley: http://www.cjnetworks.com/~shelly/notes/notes.html

15 (parentheses) 1998: a personal journal: http://www.3HarpiesLtd.com/lfeb/

16 While anyone can create home pages for loved ones, an organisation that assists

in the hosting of web sites after someone dies is Afterlife: http://www.afterlife.org.
Writes founder David Blatner on the Afterlife home page: 'Perhaps it's telling of my
Western-based culture that I was so suprised when a friend of mine asked if I would
host his web site after he died. I had simply not given any thought to the problem of
what happens to a site after someone passes away or can no longer support it for
health reasons. This man had put several years of work into his web site, and it had
become an archive of his life's musings and beliefs. He felt (and feels) strongly that
this material should remain available to people after he is no longer around to share
it, and there is no reason why this shouldn't be possible. The site takes up little
space, requires no real maintenance, and holds a treasure-trove of wonderful writing
that will probably never see its way into print....I was honored that my friend asked
me to protect something so precious to him, and I willingly agreed. But I wonder how
many people's sites are simply being 'turned off' when they no longer have a voice
(or a checkbook) to sustain them. I keep thinking: If my grandparents had built a web
site, wouldn't I want it archived and available on the net in the years to come for my
grandchildren?'

CHAPTER FIVE

The Electronic Reader

Within all the razzle dazzle, the heady and intoxicating rush and excitement, the cyber-pyrotechnics of the electronic publishing bazaar, it is easy to lose sight of the end user, the electronic reader. Yet as a new generation emerges that is becoming more used to reading on-screen than on paper, there are not only huge social and cultural questions that must be addressed but also fundamental considerations as to the types and style of content that are best served electronically on the web.

The information 'haves' and the cyber-illiterate

When Gutenberg perfected moveable type, his invention was launched on a world that was largely illiterate and thus profoundly indifferent to its implications. The medieval paradigm centred on the Church, where learning and knowledge, as represented by the hand-crafted manuscript containing ancient and medieval texts, remained in the hands of an élite that inhabited a separate world from the rest of society. The Internet, in its earliest days, remained the domain of a similar and exclusive élite, at first the military, scientific, government and academic communities who were privileged both to know of its very existence and to be able to master the arcane protocols upon which it was based.

But just as moveable type led eventually to the creation of secular and vernacular texts and in the process encouraged the rise of a literate middle class (a slow process that did not come about for centuries), so has the Internet, through its most accessible protocol, the World Wide Web, helped to create and empower a new class of computer literate users. In spite of what its most enthusiastic proponents claim, that base of users has not yet reached critical mass and the web is still a long way from being able to claim itself a universal mainstream global publishing and communications medium, as is, say the ubiquitous television which finds its way even into the tin-roofed shanty towns of the developing world, or the telephone, a communications tool that we now take almost wholly for granted.

While the demographics of web use are changing by the day if not the hour, it is nonetheless important to consider the emerging picture of the end user, the electronic reader, as well as those less fortunate, the techno-underclass or cyber-illiterate that remain cut off from web access, for whatever reason or reasons. A digital divide undoubtedly exists, and it is not an exaggeration to say that it could grow into an unbridgeable chasm, a society and indeed a world of information 'haves' and 'have nots'. For if the web empowers individuals and organisations, the converse is that those not so empowered may find themselves at a positive disadvantage.

Naturally, wealthy individuals, wealthy segments of society and wealthy countries have a considerable advantage over the poor, and such disparities are even more marked and apparent in the developing and Third World countries. The chasm between haves and have nots, however, does not just divide between rich and poor. High-powered middle-aged and older individuals with no shortage of disposable income, for example, may remain hesitant to learn about the Internet due to technophobia, the fear of being unable to grasp simple techniques, technologies and processes that are easily mastered by infant school children. Demographic studies, furthermore, have discovered patterns in web use based on gender, age, occupation, geographical location, and many other variables that are of significance.

In the early days of the web, the 1st GVU WWW Users' Survey,[1] undertaken in January 1994, discovered for example that some 94 per cent of users were male and some 56 per cent were between the ages of 21 and 30; 45 per cent described themselves as professionals and some 22 per cent as graduate students. It can be seen, with the benefit of hindsight, that these figures reflected the fact that at that time the web was in its infancy, few in so-called mainstream society either knew about or had direct access to the web while those that did probably connected through either their office computer or over an academic network. The degree of technical proficiency required to get connected in those days, moreover, meant that web use was relatively limited to that select élite who could figure out how to get the thing up and running, an exclusive club, it seems, that consisted almost entirely of young, technologically competent males.

The perception of the web as the preserve of young white male computer 'geeks' was probably born from such early studies, and the stereotype has been a hard one to shake off. However, the 8th GVU WWW Users' Survey,[2] undertaken at the end of 1997, paints a quite different emerging picture: the gender ratio has now moved closer to parity, with nearly 40 per cent of respondents being female. On the other hand, European respondents continue to be predominantly male (78 per cent).

Other impressions, for example that the web excludes minorities or the elderly, are not wholly born out by more recent studies. A survey conducted by Lou Harris and Baruch College, published in the April/May 1998 issue of the

Public Perspective, reports that as of the end of 1997, 'almost equal percentages of whites (30 per cent), African Americans (27 per cent), and Hispanics (26 per cent) logged onto the web.'[3] The same organisation reported in August 1997 that some 45 per cent of 'netizens' are over the age of 40 and 19 per cent are 50 or older. A survey by Harris Poll published in February 1998 suggests that 8 per cent of adults age 65 or over are on-line. The myth that minorities and the elderly are excluded from the World Wide Web, at least in the United States where most of these studies originate, does not seem to be wholly born out by these latest statistics. Indeed, in the case of senior citizens, this group is one of the fastest-growing segments of the on-line population, which is perhaps understandable, given that the retired may have both no shortage of disposable income as well as time on their hands to master new skills, plus the motivation of learning about the World Wide Web as a means of being less isolated in a mobile society where families may no longer live in proximity. This trend certainly seems set to continue.

It is, of course, nonsense to pretend that gaps between rich and poor, urban and rural, white and blue collar, black and white and yellow and brown, developed and developing, old and young, English- and non-English-speaking no longer exist. Whatever the changing, shifting picture of demographic patterns of web access and use, what is certain is that the digital divide remains a real one that will not easily or quickly be bridged. One only has to consider how most people access the web today, that is through a PC – a relatively large, bulky and expensive piece of technical equipment that sits on a desk in an office or a home office, not in the living room – to realise the great number of people who, for whatever reason or reasons, remain excluded from the club, indifferent to or even unaware of developments in that digital nether-region we call cyberspace. It is as well when considering the needs and requirements of the electronic reader to be just as aware of who isn't as well as who is connected and to remember that those who make up the cyber-illiterate may not necessarily always be who you imagine them to be.

The act of reading

Is the act of reading content on-screen itself essentially different to reading printed matter?

Worrying practical differences must be acknowledged. Recent usability studies, notably by Jakob Nielson and John Morkes,[4] claim that most people don't even read content on the web. Writes Nielson, 'People rarely read web pages word by word; instead, they scan the page, picking out individual words and sentences. In a recent study John Morkes and I found that 79 per cent of our test users always scanned any new page they came across; only 16 per cent read word-by-word.'[5] Nielson concludes from his research that web content needs to be 'concise, scannable, and objective.'[6]

Consider some differences between reading text on printed paper and on-screen on the web. The act of reading a book is essentially a private communion between reader and author, the engagement with a text to a certain extent a retreat from the outside world into that inner vision of the novel or text that is literally in hand. Indeed this can be a retreat that can be so utterly complete that the reader, curled up on a sofa or amidst the bustle and cacophony of, say, an airport waiting lounge, can shut out all else and actually become intimately and thoroughly immersed within the lives and world of the characters or story.

The act of reading that same content on-screen, that is, in front of a digitised flickering pattern on a computer monitor would by its very nature be less intimate, less private than the cosy act of curling up to read a book. The computer screen, at any rate, is not conducive to reading long blocks of text, as any who have tried it will confirm. Reading on-screen is eye-fatiguing, and it is not easy to follow lines down the screen. Digital type on-screen, moreover, is low resolution and lacks the subtlety and fixity of typeset print. More importantly, the computer screen, even the laptop computer screen, is something of a bulky object that is fixed in place: you cannot take it into the bath or bed comfortably to read and the office-associated nature of the instrument inevitably imparts a business-like aura to material so accessed. The elusive sometimes unconscious process of losing oneself completely within the intimate covers of a book, within the world created by a single author, is quite simply not possible through a computer screen.[7]

It is not the process of concentration that is altered, it is the essentially private act of engagement with a single author that is somehow not possible. Of course, few argue that the web is an ideal medium for the delivery and access of novels or other lengthy texts. But it is not only the type of content on which the medium itself has an impact, it is the act of accessing content itself. Material that is delivered and accessed by way of the World Wide Web invites a many-to-many connectivity that is essentially the antithesis of the one-to-one engagement of reader/author. This process can take the reader into more public realms that, if not always demanding a response, nonetheless often invite one. In the process, the essential balance of the role between reader and writer, as well as reader and other readers, has been shifted.

Though many may bemoan the loss of private intercourse and communion between author and reader, it should also be acknowledged that in a positive way, readers can become, in some instances, even partners in the collaboration and creation of a work. They are often positively invited to contribute, to give feedback, even to create their own content. The impermanence of content on the web – often here today and literally gone tomorrow – means that content is no longer carved in stone, as it were, or fixed in printed type. The ease with which content can be altered, amended, changed, or obliterated means that the fixity of the printed word, and to a certain extent, the univocal authority of the author has been diminished. At the same time the reader has been empowered to participate, either through direct feedback to the author, or through involvement and engagement with other readers.

In this sense, certainly, the electronic reader differs fundamentally from his counterpart accessing text only through print: the former interactive, and engaged publicly, the latter more contemplative, finding connections, relationships and meaning in an inner, private communion between reader and author.

Navigating cyberspace

It should be acknowledged, therefore, that the new medium often may not lend itself to traditional texts that have been and will continue to be delivered best in the form of the printed book. The novel as we know it came about, after all, only with the rise and proliferation of printed secular matter which was made possible with the perfection of the printing press. The concentration and varied pace with which the reader engages such texts is facilitated by the portability of the book, which can be carried around anywhere, picked up and read in short bursts, or over long extended periods of hours and days. Should a passage not be clear, then the reader can re-read it or pause to look up words in a dictionary.

Reading content accessed on the web, by contrast, is always something of a twitchy and frenetic exercise, especially in those countries, the UK and most of Europe, for example, where users feel that the metre, the charge for local phone calls, which is still very high, is always ticking. Even if accessing the web were free (as it is in the US, for example, with free local phone calls), the very nature of hypertext positively invites the reader to click on highlighted words or images that take them elsewhere. The term 'surfing the web' has come from 'channel surfing', that twitchiest of all activities whereby the proverbial couch potato, fortified with gallons of soft drinks, cans of beer, and junk food, armed with remote control in hand, moves endlessly and restlessly between terrestrial, cable and satellite channels, rarely pausing to watch anything in its entirety, and rarely, it seems, ever satisfied.

Channel surfing is almost wholly random, however; the truly dedicated and mindless surfer simply pushes the 'next' button robotically, running through the

channels not by logic or interest but as they appear in order. The web surfer, at least, is driven by hypertext links that are based in part on association, links connecting with interrelated links. But the danger remains the same: it is easy for the electronic reader to get lost, to get side-tracked on new topics, and to rarely be able to complete an entire document before moving restlessly elsewhere. The act of reading hypertext, therefore, requires the mastering of new skills, and perhaps in the future the development of new aids and tools, in order to keep track of a thread of an argument, and not become sidelined by links that take you out and beyond, inviting you to forget why or where you were in the first place.

Horizontal associations versus vertical depth

The most effective hypertext documents usually contain plenty of hyperlinks, those bits of highlighted text or images that when clicked take the reader elsewhere. A hypertext document that does not make use of such links, by contrast, is one that is not making full use of the unique power of this medium. The inclusion of hyperlinks, in granting the potential to add considerable auxiliary, complementary, and supplementary information, leads to a different way of experiencing content for the electronic reader.

Let's consider an example of how this works: take the cornerstone of Western literature, Homer's *Odyssey*, (interestingly a text that came originally from the oral, non-written tradition). The Homer homepage[8] indicates that there are various versions of the text on-line, including the classic translation by George Chapman.[9] There are links to pages that give background on the Homeric gods[10] and the Trojan war;[11] there is a link to a site which includes images from vase paintings and other classical artefacts depicting the Homeric world;[12] and naturally there are academic studies and Homer projects.[13] There are annotated bibliographies, literary criticism essays, a site that draws links between the *Odyssey* and the movie *2001, a Space Odyssey*,[14] chat and bulletin boards as well as live recitation chat rooms, and links to the island of Ithaka together with a map and tourist information, the Greek National Tourist Board, and much else. These examples demonstrate the power of hypertext to link relevant associated primary and secondary material and in the process to amplify knowledge.

However, the question needs to be asked: for the reader, the lover of classical literature, the student of the *Odyssey*, are such links strictly necessary, or indeed, can they instead prove something of an irresistible distraction? It could well be argued that close reading of the text is far more important than secondary and auxiliary information, that this freer, associative, non-linear approach to a text leads to a more fragmented, possibly less critical and rigorous approach to literature. I can understand both arguments, but confess to being ultimately seduced by the power of hypertext to fill in the voids, add so much more of interest to the larger picture (even if not strictly relevant), in the process amplifying knowledge of a place, an historic period, art and culture, and domestic daily life, even though I am aware that such knowledge may not be strictly necessary to experience the sheer power and wonder of the narrative itself, which after all has endured for some 3000 years with no need of such auxiliary aids.

For is not the process of learning, to a great extent, the process of creating such relationships for ourselves? Just as one can no more gain a deep and real understanding of a text by reading abridged crib or study notes, so lies the risk that the over reliance on hypertext links to form and provide such relationships may rob the electronic reader of an essential element in the thinking and learning process. I have myself often fallen into this trap, a process that begins with the excitement of using a directory or search engine to find related material that inevitably leads to further related material. Clicking a link to see what is available, relevant, and reliable inevitably leads one further and further from one's original search, but the quest to examine, to discover what might be is completely and totally irresistible. In the process, one visits a number of related sites, rarely pausing long enough to examine any of them critically, and in the end, at best you are left with a list of bookmarked links which need to be re-examined again, while at worst, in one's almost orgasmic and uncontrollable state of excitement, the clicks have come too fast, the bookmarked trails of interest left incomplete, lost forever in the dense and unnavigable forest that requires you to start virtually at the beginning again.

As the web of content becomes ever more entangled and complicated, as the need to find effective ways of organising and searching for content intensifies, a new form of content is emerging to service the needs of the electronic reader, so-called meta-forms that consists of little more than collections of related hypertext links. Yahoo!,[15] the most visited site on the World Wide Web, is just such a meta-form, a directory, or in other words, an information filter made up of no more than collections of links, registered into categories and sub-categories to assist the reader in finding organised content. There are scores of other examples which serve to filter information, making sense out of unmanageable chaos. Indeed, would the World Wide Web in its present form be possible without the search engine or directory? We've already come to rely on it like a crutch, to help us stand up straight against the overwhelming deluge of available information that sometimes threatens to overwhelm us. For indeed we've already reached a point where we have at our virtual fingertips more information than our minds are able to process.

The danger is that in the process a new generation will grow up that can no longer understand the need to be able to think and concentrate in an applied linear fashion, but rather will believe instead that links and relationships between subjects and disciplines can be supplied by meta-form directories, specialised search engines, intelligent agents and other sources. Thus the mental skills that have traditionally been central to the learning process will gradually wither and atrophy, like some vestigial mental appendix that through evolution has become surplus to our day-to-day requirements. The result could be that individuals find that they have the capacity to acquire an endless wealth of factual knowledge (or, more pertinently, the ability to access and reference it from computers) without the necessary understanding or wisdom that has always been fundamental to the relational learning process.

Information overload, unreliability and web litter

We may, ultimately, be able to let our computers do the thinking, just as a generation ago we learned to let our fingers do the walking when the telephone was 'cutting edge' technology. It is just as well to remember, however, that the electronic, computerised processing of digital information is not in its essence really all that wise or intelligent. Make no mistake, the capacity to process bits – digital pulses of 'on' or 'off' electricity – is powerful indeed, and can help us to bring complex and distant relationships to the fore, find related sites through keyword searches, even to a certain extent help filter that information through ever finer sieves. At some point, however, the source content itself needs to be accessed and processed by the human brain – there is not yet a computer that will do this for us!

Yet how, in a world where content is self-proliferating like the proverbial cyber-rabbit, is the electronic reader supposed to make sense of it all, and not fall victim to information overload? This is one of the great challenges that now faces us. In that former, more certain world that existed before the World Wide Web, institutions – schools, universities, churches, governments, central broadcasting organisations such as the BBC – helped us to process such information, imparting criteria and values that guided us to distinguish between that which was valid and reliable and that which was ersatz or even downright spurious. Such criteria no doubt may have had a top heavy cultural bias based on the traditional canon of western thought, learning, and culture, the so-called 'dead white male syndrome'.

But now, in the many-to-many paradigm that is the World Wide Web, where anybody can be an author/publisher, where narrowcasting to specialised and ever smaller niche audiences is replacing the concept of national broadcasting, with all the collective resonance which that implies, where that same canon of western thought has been replaced by a multi-cultural, many-faceted opus that represents the fragmentation of our post-modern condition, the end result is that we live increasingly in an age of ever greater uncertainty. The paradox seems to be that we may well find ourselves suddenly information rich yet spiritually and morally bankrupt, void of guiding principles and values.

This same lack of any central guiding concept, values or control lies at the very heart of the web, indeed was central to its creation, thus ensuring for the paranoic military who created it that it could never be dominated or destroyed. There are those who would like to impose controls on the web, limit what can and cannot be published on it, and in the process impose some overriding set of central values. Freedom of expression, on the other hand, seems likely to win out, not least because it is so difficult to put any such controls effectively in place.

Yet at the same time, this anarchic side of the web seems to reflect a medium that is at best uncontrollable, at worst downright untrustworthy. In the ancient world, when words were carved in stone, they carried by sheer physical weight something of the authority of a decree. Similarly, the process and expense of manufacture and distribution granted authority (something rightly or wrongly) to the printed word, especially in the form of the book. However, now that publishing on the web can be carried out by just about anyone with access to a computer and a modem, at the most minimal expense, when words, as weightless as light, appear and disappear one day from the next, when the ever-changing screenscape of the digital word has by its very nature a sense of impermanence, does the electronic reader, unconsciously perhaps, place less value and importance to the word accessed on-screen as opposed to print? More to the point, when words and text and endless screens of information are available for free, do we subconsciously value that information less?

When information is a scarce commodity, available only to those with either the intellectual or financial means to track it down or buy it, then it remains the realm of a privileged élite. When information is freely available to all, and when anybody can simply use an intelligent agent to find it for him, then are we wrong to be cautious or wary of it?

The craft of book production grew from a tradition where books were scarce and valuable objects in their own right, regardless of the information or texts they contained. The inexpensive (to produce as well as to purchase) mass market paperback, when it first appeared, led to the creation of new genres of content, lighter, less serious than the more permanent gravitas found within the leather bound hardback. Paperbacks were books to read on the beach while on holiday, and to simply discard – give away to someone else, or just leave in the holiday apartment – once you'd finished them. Content on the web similarly is so cheap that as a result it is sometimes treated with lazy contempt, even by its very creators. Witness the increase in web litter, sites whose useful life has expired, whose content is hopelessly out of date but which are left on servers all the same out of sheer laziness, eating up valuable bandwidth and attracting the attention of robot search engines that catalogue them, thus adding to the unreliability of their results. When server space is so cheap, human time at so high a premium, it is likely that such web litter will ever increase and never be cleaned up, simply because it is not cost effective to do so. As this problem compounds and builds up over the coming years, it has the potential to pose serious problems to the whole system.

Content and the electronic reader

Those who create content, then, need to remain aware above all of their audience, the electronic readers of today and tomorrow. But if the demographics of web access remain ever-shifting and too difficult to focus on precisely – the snapshot picture taken today or yesterday already out of date by tomorrow – one still needs to give thought as much to those who are likely to be connected as to those who remain excluded. Until global critical mass is reached, something which is unlikely to happen for years still, I conjecture, then the medium's less than universal access has considerable implications for the creation of local and regional content as well as non-English content.

For if the power of the medium lies in its ability to cast content far and wide, in the process connecting and creating communities of shared interest, by contrast, one of its weaknesses is its inability, at present, to serve small local communities effectively, save for those isolated and exceptional areas, mostly in the USA, that are almost wholly connected and on-line. Urban, regional, and non-English speaking national content suffers as a result, and will continue to lag behind, the creators of such content waiting ever more impatiently for their specific markets to grow, to reach neighbourhood critical mass. Make no mistake, that demographic user base is growing, but overall this growth is on a global basis: it may still be difficult to attract a significant base of users from small local areas, towns, cities, regions or even countries.

The danger, then, is that inevitably the medium coerces us into speaking to each other in the lowest common denominator in the quest to find a language, a common ground, that we all understand. Content creators must decide whether or not to produce web sites that will reach the largest audience (including those technologically challenged still using the oldest browser versions), or instead seek to produce more snazzy sites that are only accessible by those whose browsers support the latest features. And the electronic reader? My conjecture is that as the user base grows globally, local, regional and non-English national content will ultimately increase simply because users will prefer it to more generic, US-centric English language content that currently dominates the web. But since the medium's greatest power remains its ability to reach global audiences who share interests and speak a common language, it seems certain that English as the *lingua franca* of the web is set to continue.

The lesson seems to be that the electronic reader may not only need to master an entirely new way of accessing information by way of hypertext and hyperlinks, the non-English speaking reader may also need to learn to read, write, perhaps even speak a new language in order to take fullest advantage of what we egocentrically call the world's most powerful 'global medium'. And while we easily bandy claims about the web's ability to reach global audiences numbering in the millions, it is just as well to remember that few sites actually do. Rather, it would seem that being focused on and aware of the specific and particular needs and requirements of the electronic reader – your reader – is about the most we can hope to do.

1 Results from the 1st World Wide Web Users' Survey undertaken by the Graphics, Visualization, & Usability Center (GVU), Georgia Tech College of Computing in January 1994. The GVU surveys of web use are among the longest running of such studies. At the time of writing, the latest study is the 10th WWW User Survey (October 1998), but later studies will certainly be available by the time this book is published. Results of all the surveys are available on the GVU web site: http://www.cc.gatech.edu/gvu/user_surveys/

2 The 9th GVU WWW User Survey confirms this trend: as stated in the Executive Summary of the survey: 'The general demographics of the user population moved closer to the characteristics of the general population with a continued increase in the proportion of female users.' 9th GVU WWW User Survey: http://www.cc.gatech.edu/gvu/user_surveys/survey-1998-04/

3 These figures come from an article by Brock N. Meeks, MSNBC, 'The population of Web users is now nearly identical to the statistical makeup of the United States', as reported by ZDNN News Channel, 30 April 1998: http://www.zdnn.com

4 Research study by Jakob Nielson and John Morkes for the SunSoft Science Office, April 1997, as reported on the web site 'Writing for the Web':
http://www.useit.com/papers/webwriting/
5 Jakob Nielson's Alert Box for 1 October 1997:
http://www.useit.com/alertbox/9710a.html
6 These ideas and conclusions are explored further in another article by Nielson and Morkes entitled 'Concise, Scannable, and Objective: How to Write for the Web':
http://www.useit.com/papers/webwriting/writing.html
7 That is not to say that one can't lose oneself almost completely on-screen while accessing content on the World Wide Web: many of us do so with frightening regularity and rapidity. But but few would argue that the essential act of engagement between the web content creator and the electronic reader is the same as that which takes place through the thoughtful reading of printed text.
8 The Homer Homepage:
http://www.dc.peachnet.edu/~shale/humanities/literature/world_literature/homer.html
9 The Odyssey, translated by George Chapman:
http://www.columbia.edu/acis/bartleby/chapman/
10 The Homeric Gods: http://www.usask.ca/classics/CourseNotes/HomBA.html
11 The Trojan War (includes summary of Trojan war story, and passage from Thucydides on the war): http://home5.swipnet.se/~w-58907/GGGM-F/TrojanWar.html
12 The Trojan War images from vase paintings and other classical artefacts from European paintings, compiled by Ora Zehavi and Dr. Sonia Klinger, University of Haifa: http://www-lib.haifa.ac.il/www/art/troyan.html
13 Homer projects include Homerica, a project from the University of Grenoble: http://ull-doc.u-grenoble3.fr/stendhal/homerica/ and The Odyssey Project, an archaeological project founded by Prof. Sarantis Symeonoglou to determine the relationship between the ancient remains on the island of Ithaka and the Ithaka detailed in Homer's Odyssey: http://www.artsci.wustl.edu/~ssymeono/index.html
14 Parallels between the Odyssey and the film 2001:
http://adhocalypse.arts.unimelb.edu.au/fcf/ucr/student/1996/a.coulter/hot/2001.htm
15 Yahoo!: http://www.yahoo.com

PART TWO

Creating Content on the World Wide Web

CHAPTER SIX

Hypertext

Hypertext is the heart, by association pumping lifeblood to the aortae, arteries and capillaries that so linked and nurtured create the network of networks that is the World Wide Web. In order to produce creative and effective content on the web, it is essential to forget for a moment about all those other singing and dancing features that make up today's web sites and consider instead the fundamental question of how hypertext functions, and how the act of conceiving and creating hypertext differs from that of creating traditional linear text.

The hypertext document is by nature and definition complex and potentially powerful. The most exciting fundamental feature of web content – in spite of animations, Shockwave, javascript gizmos and whatever else is the current flavour of the month on the web when you read this – still remains the link, the essential building block of the web: that bit of highlighted, coloured or underlined text which, when clicked, takes you, more or less instantly depending on how lucky you are, on a magical mystery tour to another document that can even reside on a computer located on the other side of the earth. The best web sites consist of collections of such hypertext documents, each an individual knowledge domain or node, all cross-referenced and cross-linked, held together by lateral associations and relationships. Such collections can in effect go on forever, like a game of chinese whispers, subtly and gradually leading to new forms and meanings. The hyperlink that takes the reader to a related document on another web site itself leads to further links on that site, and to others on further related sites, each connected in some way to the original, no matter how distant or far-fetched that connection eventually becomes.

Hypertext has been described as 'non-sequential reading and writing...allowing authors to link information, create paths through a corpus of related material, annotate existing texts, create notes and point readers to either bibliographical data or the body of the referenced text.'[1] Another definition asserts that 'hypertext is a system of knowledge representation in which elements of knowledge can be assembled in different ways according to the different perspectives of the user.'[2] Both definitions point to the inherently multifarious nature of hypertext: it can be both created and accessed in a non-sequential or non-linear fashion, and its ultimate structure and assembly involves acts on the part of both the content creator and the user, who is free to choose not only in what order to explore elements of content, but also what parts to access and what to ignore. The implications of this are profound, for in a very real sense, hypertext involves the relinquishing of control over the final form of content into the hands of the user.

The construction of a hypertext document is thus very different from the construction of a traditional, sequential or linear text. However, this process should by no means be seen as a less considered activity, the haphazard, willy-nilly creation of links that can be accessed in any order whatsoever. Though on first glance, many web sites may appear seemingly random in structure, inviting the user to go anywhere, the well constructed web site manages its complexity in such a way that the user is aided in where to go and thus does not end up helplessly and hopelessly lost in cyberspace. Indeed, structure and navigation are fundamental to the effective creation of complex hypertext documents.

Metaphors and hypertext

If, as outlined in the previous chapter, accessing hypertext places new demands on the user, so does the creation of effective hypertext documents similarly require a new approach, indeed, an entirely different conceptualisation of that content itself. How to grasp, glimpse, pin down the sometimes ephemeral nature of the hypertext document or collection of documents, so much more difficult to hold on to, to conceptualise than the reassuring solidity of linear thoughts set down on paper and print. In a medium that is rooted in metaphor, that rhetorical figure of speech may help the content creator to conceptualise the form and forms of hypertext. Let's consider, then, for a moment a few such metaphors.

The image of a web itself is certainly one of the most visually compelling metaphors that illustrates the finely interconnected nature of a hypertext document, at once demonstrating its non-linear shape and structure, as well as its delicate, sometimes evanescent, almost invisible nature. Like a web, the hypertext document is something that is intricately constructed or contrived, a complex structure often lacking a true centre, the delicate whole held together by its inherent collective strength rather than by any individual pillars or solid foundation. Like a web on a child's climbing frame, it is possible to scramble from one point to the other by any number of different routes, either directly from point A to point B, around the periphery, or by any other roundabout means. A spider's web, of course, exists to ensnare. Similarly, the hypertext document attracts its users not through a single door of entry but by whatever means and direction of entry they choose to utilise; and links furthermore catch the unwary, often leading to an evermore entangled destination that was perhaps not the original goal.

The act of accessing hypertext documents is likened to surfing. What does this imply? That there is a sea of knowledge, information, and entertainment out there as deep and profound as the oceans, a great bottomless pool that we can access, if only we have the beach-savvy skills to catch and ride the waves of content as they come rolling in. The surfer's success at catching a wave, however, depends not just on his own skills, but also on the chance waves that happen to come his way. The act of surfing the web can be just as fortuitous and serendipitous an experience, the success or failure at finding a site or related sites often seemingly dictated by invisible factors and forces outside one's control.

The content creator needs to be aware of this in order to assist the surfer as much as possible. Indeed, in web publishing, as much care and attention needs to be given not just to the construction of a hypertext document, but also to the process by which users will find and access that document. By understanding this process – the use of search engines and directories, links and reciprocal links with other sites, e-mail, newsgroups and discussion lists, as well as the internal navigation of a hypertext document itself – and by the intelligent use of metatags (invisible information on site description and key words which is placed in the header of HTML documents), content creators can at least ensure that they have done as much as possible to enable the casual web surfer to find their site and hop on for a ride.[3]

In many way, though, the surfing metaphor is not an apt one at all. The image that it actually brings up is not of some cool dude hanging ten on a malibu board but rather instead of some spaced-out telly addict, fingers restlessly and uncontrollably twitching on the remote control every minute or two. The web surfer equivalent, by extension, perches glassy-eyed in front of a computer monitor, mindlessly clicking on any bit of coloured text to zoom off to the next hyperdocument, without ever attempting to make sense of what is already on the screen. There is a certain degree of truth in this stereotype, and it should be acknowledged that there is something inherent in the hypertext document itself that seems to encourage positively such a restless at best, mindless at worst, approach to accessing content.

But there is a significant difference between the channel surfer and the web surfer. The former merely runs through the endless choices before him at random, whilst the web surfer, by comparison, at least clicks on hyperlinks that have a degree of lateral association and relationships between each other. And it is the content creator who has put in those links in the first place – they don't just happen to appear there by chance. Thus, though the content creator may have little control over directing where the user eventually ends up, considerable thought can be given as to what links are included in a hyperdocument, whether or not they are really necessary and help to amplify content, or whether or not they are a distraction that simply leads the user away from the core of the content.

Perhaps a more apt metaphor for the act of accessing hypertext documents is that of a journey. Certainly, a book can be a journey. The author takes the reader somewhere outside himself. But in such an instance, it is the author who controls and steers that journey, taking the reader to an ultimate destination that is the author's intended conclusion. A web site, by contrast, made up of collections of internal and external linked knowledge nodes or domains, on the other hand, takes the reader in unexpected directions and to destinations that not even the content creator can usually anticipate. Like the traveller poised at the crossroads, having to choose alternative routes that lead to different destinations, the web traveller may find himself equally at the point of embarkation on a journey full of inchoate potential. Hypertext represents a complex network of different roads to take or to leave, and it is often the journey itself, not necessarily any ultimate destination, that is most exciting for both content creator and user as well. In a real sense, it is as if the content creator has given the user a map and subsequently left him to go where he chooses, even to links or places that extend beyond the edges of that particular cartographic folio. The different conceptual mentality that this imposes on the creation of content is, or should be, considerable.

Given the ephemeral nature of hypertext and the web site, and that metaphors are useful in helping to conceptualise how it differs essentially from more traditional media, it is perhaps not surprising that visual and structural metaphors themselves are widely and often effectively used to identify web sites themselves. Indeed, as web sites have evolved from hierarchical, mainly text-led directories of hyperlinks to more visually complex and interesting constructions, the use of such metaphors has become a feature of the mature web site.

Take the idea of a 'virtual café', for example. Real cafés should be warm places that make you want to visit them. More than that, the best can become almost second homes, the sort where your *cappuccino* is made and on the counter virtually the minute you come through the door, your seat by the window and rack of newspapers always vacant and awaiting you. Cafés are places to hang out in, to think and write, to meet people, either friends or new acquaintances, to kill time and just relax. It's no wonder that they can make such compelling metaphors for web sites and in the process engender a warm sense of community and belonging.

Such community metaphors can be rich in suggestion and meaning that goes beyond the obvious. The concept of a 'virtual mall', for example, is suggestive of the real archetypal shopping mall that exists in virtually every city, town and small village throughout the USA. Far more than simply some vast commercial conglomeration of shops and boutiques grouped together under one roof, the physical space of the mall engenders a sense of community, a destination in itself that brings young and old together for entertainment, to meet friends or dates, to eat or drink, to partake in physical recreation or sporting activity, or simply to pass time, as well as to make purchases from the vast array of shops. The best shopping web sites may similarly be those that endeavour to become such virtual communities by offering content that goes far beyond the mere facility to make on-line purchases and in the process brings together people with shared interests and values.

Perhaps because the web is still so relatively new and there remains a certain perceived resistance to it, some content creators borrow metaphors from traditional media. The concept of web channels, for example, is immediately familiar to everyone, though in reality there is a considerable difference between television which broadcasts programmes usually once only (forgetting for the moment reruns, which we never know when will reappear like last night's regurgitated TV dinner) and so-called netcasts on the web, web content which, even when broadcast live, are usually archived and thus can be accessed by anyone at any time. Other web sites choose to try and emulate the form and appearance of glossy magazines or daily newspapers, to lesser or greater degrees of success. And there are now even web stations that broadcast Internet radio and video live, though the technological problems in doing so over limited bandwidth still leaves much to be desired compared to the original media.

As the web evolves, it is probable that we will need to continue to invent new metaphors in our attempt to define it, whether borrowed from spatial, mechanical, geographical, natural, or architectural concepts. The need to use and create new metaphors to help define, shape and construct the web is perhaps understandable in these early days when we are all still trying to come to terms with the new medium, to grasp and understand and, yes, visualise the cyberspace that lies beyond our computer monitors. We live, after all, in a physical world, where we are used to watching the box, holding a book, turning the pages of a magazine or newspaper. It is ultimately the sheer ephemeral nature of the hypertext documents that make up the web which we all still find at once so exciting yet as well, at times, so very troubling.

The act of browsing hypertext

If the comparison with channel surfing is less than helpful in defining how the user accesses a hypertext document or documents, it may still be useful to consider how the act of browsing is an inherent and essential element of the process of exploring and discovering hypertext. The Index or Welcome page of a web site usually (though not always) is like a shop window, inviting the user to inspect the the various categories or choices of linked chunks of content that hypertext represents and indeed, if sufficiently interested, to enter through the front door to browse awhile. This act of browsing is quite unlike accessing linear text, for it involves a sometimes focused and systematic, sometimes serendipitous following of an idea or related ideas or concepts to associated links that lead to other related links and finally to the various chunks of information themselves.

Naturally there may be many different types of browsing strategies that are adopted by users. The manner in which a user approaches the act of browsing content depends on many factors, including the motive for the search. Is the user purposefully seeking specific information, following links in a more freely associative manner, or merely roaming at random, for example. Such motives may determine different strategies for exploring hypertext. Large areas of content may be scanned superficially without ever going in depth into any one area in order to see the broad extent of what is available. Or else a subject may be delved into ever more deeply in order to penetrate and find particular or precise information. Browsing in a more freely associative manner is another approach whereby a great deal of material is accessed in order to arrive at an answer to or solution for a question or problem.

The act of learning, furthermore, often involves simply wandering or wading through material in an unstructured, sometimes repetitive pattern without an initial fixed idea, motive or destination in mind. In many instances, users adopt a hybrid approach to browsing, for example, setting out with a clear and fixed intention to find specific and precise material, but getting sidetracked or distracted along the way, and so ending up exploring other material more serendipitously or less systematically. Even with the best intentions in the world, the nature of browsing hypertext means that the user often ends up, at best, in places not originally envisaged, at worst, hopelessly lost.

The content creator cannot be expected to foresee the motives or intentions of visitors to a web site, but the way that a site is structured will often dictate how it is explored. Indeed, the well structured site that considers its users and their reasons for visiting a site can positively facilitate the act of browsing.

Hypertext structure and non-linear paradigms

While the typical web site may consist of collections of hypertext documents that are all linked and cross-linked to each other, there are still many different ways in which each site may be structured. The correct structure for each depends on a number of factors, including its main purpose, its target audience, as well as the type, style and extent of content that it contains.

Already there has been an evolution in hypertext structure. Some of the earliest web sites, for example, evolved from existing hierarchical telnet and gopher directories at academic, government and other institutions. Such sites, often functional in content and form, offered a Home or Welcome page that did little more than list a range of hyperlinks for further exploration. Indeed, it is surprising how many sites still follow this basic model even now (including some of the most visited search directories, though in fairness, a directory is one example where this model is most effective, and indeed such flatness is usually just the tip of a profoundly deep iceberg of content buried beneath the numerous category headings). On a large site, such a list can run for several screens, resulting in a flat structure with scores of links that may be difficult to make sense of. In many instances, the various hyperdocuments that lead off from the main Index page may not necessarily be cross-linked to each other, but rather require a return to the central index by means of a Home button. This flat structure, though rather pedantic and unimaginative in form, has one considerable advantage: most of the site's content can be viewed and accessed directly from its first or opening pages, without the need to navigate through a host of other pages before getting there.

A site structured vertically, on the other hand, may offer only a handful of options on the Welcome or Index page, but each of these sections may itself lead to a further host of levels buried ever deeper within the hyperdocument, each of which progressively adds greater in-depth, detailed or complementary information and knowledge. This type of division-and-classification structure may in many cases seem to be the most logical and clear, depending on the content requirements. On the other hand, if insufficient clues are given on the Welcome page as to the extent and type of content available inside, then it can result in users and especially casual browsers never getting beyond that first page, simply because they don't know precisely what there is on offer (and are too lazy, stressed, pushed for time, whatever, to bother to look).

The use of navigation bars may serve as aids for web sites with this type of structure, allowing 'tables of contents' to be kept visible on the top, bottom, or sides of 'pages'. What the vertical model emphasises, however, is that structure in an effective web site ought to concern not only the logical ordering of material, but also the demonstration of that order, preferably in as clear, sometimes graphically represented, even entertaining a fashion as possible, in order to invite and entice users to access it.

Some web sites, by contrast, seek to give the appearance of lacking any formal structure whatsoever, with diverse and seemingly unrelated areas of content all cross-linked, and to be accessed in whatever order or fashion that the user so desires. Eschewing any attempt to control or guide the user on where to go, such hypertext documents can even have elements of randomness programmed into their structure, with pages of text or images rotating or being replaced on, say, the Welcome page, by the use of a javascript. In other cases, there is no obvious Welcome, Home, or entry page. Users may come to the web site through any number of doors of entry, and each chunk of content needs to be able to stand on its own, with no reference or cross-reference to any other. Such web sites, linking various and diverse knowledge and special interest domains, at times however tenuously, can be at once the most exciting or the most frustrating of all, depending on your point of view.

Though hypertext is by definition non-sequential in form and structure, it is, of course, still possible, though not necessarily desirable, to create a wholly linear web site. This can be achieved simply by offering the user no option but to proceed where the author or content creator compels him to (provided the user doesn't get fed up in the meantime and simply click elsewhere). In such instances, the first page leads to the next page which leads to the next, and so on, with no or few internal cross-references between pages or external hyperlinks. There may be instances where it is important to engage the users' attention in this fashion; a hypertext document may be offering step-by-step instructions, or it may consist of a text broken up into chunks or blocks that needs to read from front to back. Or such a linear, controlled section might form but a part of a larger site that is organised, for example, in the division-and-classification method above.

None of the above forms is necessarily better or worse than any other. Again, it is the nature and purpose of the content itself, together with the requirements of the target audience, that ultimately should be the determinant of hypertext structure. Content creators, above all, need to assist users to understand the structure of their web site, not least because no universal standards or conventions have yet emerged. Each web site may have its own unique user interface, but it is imperative that the logic and order of that particular interface is made clear and comprehensible to the user. A site map, that is a diagram that shows the branches and sub-branches of a site, may be one way of demonstrating this visually.

The hyperlink

Whatever the shape of its underlying structure or structures, the key to a strong hyperdocument lies in the effective organisation of such material through the creation of a set of links that draws together the related associations, sometimes obviously, at other times more creatively, even artistically, which collectively make up each contextual knowledge domain or node of inter-related content. If hypertext is the heart, then hyperlinks are the arteries upon which the lifeblood of each web travels. The effective use of the link, therefore, is one essential element in the construction of creative and effective content for the web.

What does the hyperlink do? Quite simply, the act of clicking on a highlighted word or a linked image takes the user somewhere else, either to another part of that same document (in the case of an anchor which, for example, can be linked to a footnote or sub-heading of the same document), to another section of the same web site, or to some external site located anywhere else in the world. This is indeed a most powerful facility, and enables rich and in-depth collections of related documents to be grouped together by association. Indeed, the lateral leaps of association that links often lead to can at times be exhilarating, even breathtaking. For anyone researching a topic for the first time, the wealth of interconnected knowledge that the medium places literally at the fingertips is quite amazing, especially when compared to how such material would have been gathered and accessed in the not so distant past, the countless treks to numerous libraries, the waiting for books or periodicals to be ordered and despatched, the time lag to access facsimile or multimedia material.

On the other hand, it must be acknowledged that the process of accessing hypertext documents by means of the link is essentially fragmentary by nature and at times not overly conducive to the considered and thoughtful working out of a singular argument or train of thought. Not only does the nature of hypertext present multi-faceted points of view to a topic or related topics, quite simply, the distractions involved in accessing hypertext are many and varied. Those coloured bits of text, those linked images, come too fast and furious even for experienced web users, and the temptation to click is almost always irresistible, and before we know it we may find ourselves immediately transported elsewhere, often to somewhere fascinating and amazing and filled with even more links, but which may have little relevance to our previous train of thought. Even as we grope for the Back button, we know that it is hopeless, that something else has already caught our eye, we click again and before we can blink, become hopelessly lost in cyberspace, unable even to remember where we were going, what we were seeking in the first place.

Presented with a screenful of links, furthermore, all ostensibly associated or related to our chosen topic of interest, how is one to distinguish the valuable from the inconsequential? Until you begin to click and examine one by one, it may be impossible to make telling judgements. And indeed, in many cases the site with valuable and authoritative information and content might be missed due to its poor and uninviting design, while a flashy site catches your attention instead, but only after exploring five or six linked documents on that site do you realise that it is totally useless, a considerable waste of time. Therefore, though powerful indeed, the hyperlink, it must be acknowledged, can at times be a mighty inefficient means of finding worthwhile content.

The hyperlink furthermore challenges such long cherished concepts as the narrative, the basic belief that a story, whether fiction, non-fiction, article, thesis or book, has a beginning, middle and an end. Many web sites can be entered from multiple doors of entry, and there is usually no definite ending to a hypertext document, with each user accessing only those elements that are of particular private interest, and in whatever order he cares to explore them before moving on and out, elsewhere by way of the hyperlink.

Indeed, the web site as a collection of hypertext documents is usually not even intended to be accessed in its entirety by most users. Thus, the concept and integrity of the whole of a work, and with it the need to read, view, understand that whole in order to gain an understanding of the author's argument or point of view, is similarly challenged. And it is the link that constantly challenges, the link or links put in by the authors themselves, constant invitations to leave and visit elsewhere.

The content creator needs, therefore, to be vigilant and remain aware above all of the end users' foibles and weaknesses, and of the essential scatty, unfocused nature of hypertext, which through the link can so easily lead one astray, or, more pertinently, away from where we want our readers to be. The temptation when creating a hypertext document is generally to put in not too few, but actually too many hyperlinks. The desire to demonstrate our cleverness, our in-depth knowledge associations, and the interconnectivity of a hypertext document by including as many highlighted or coloured bits of text as possible simply for the sake of it should be resisted wherever possible if the aim of a web site is to keep the reader's attention for as long as possible. The content creator needs to ask, therefore, if the links included are absolutely necessary; do they amplify and expand knowledge and make creative, lateral associations; or are they gratuitous, an unnecessary distraction? On the other hand, the aim of some web sites, may be precisely and simply to do no more than suggest connections and associations by offering links freely, generously and gratuitously on whatever subject or topic. If that is the case, then by all means link and link again to your heart's desire.

Organisation and navigation in hyperspace

No matter what the motives and aims of a web site, considerable thought needs to be given to the organisation and navigation of web content. For indeed, if the web site is essentially an interconnected collection of hypertext documents, one of the greatest challenges is presenting that content in a shape and manner that is accessible to the user. Say Deborah M. Edwards and Lynda Hardman:

> 'Hypertext, as well as providing us with more locations in which to store information and more dimensions in which to travel, also provides us with greater potential for becoming disoriented and lost. Clearly, locating text if the user doesn't know what is available or how to access it, is a major problem.'[4]

There are many ways that the user can be assisted to locate content. Organising material in a suitable and rational fashion is certainly one way to achieve this. An index of content, for example, can be organised alphabetically; by subject; by date with the most recent content on top; by spatial metaphor (say, a shopping mall where you enter different areas or departments); by category and sub-category; by geographic location; by placing the most important information at the top, and the least at the bottom, and so on. Various combinations can be used together, geographical or subject content, for example, leading to lists that are organised alphabetically. Different sections of the same site might utilise different methods of content organisation and presentation.

Studies have attempted to identify some of the most effective ways of helping the user to navigate hyperspace. Edwards and Hardman suggest that spatially-based navigation devices, that is, those that 'present the information structure in a 2- or 3-dimensional form'[5] may be the most effective. Lesley Allinson and Nick Hammond are in accord with Edwards and Hardman on the effective use of spatial metaphors:

> 'Comparisons and analogies between the virtual world of the hyperdocument and the real world of everyday experience allows users to construct a more accurate mental model of what to expect from the hypertext. Work in this field supports the idea that metaphors in general, and the travel metaphor in particular, are extremely powerful aids to navigation around complex data structures such as hypertext systems.'[6]

Just as traditional printed material utilises page furniture such as running heads and folios to help the reader know where he is, so does the web have its own devices for navigating hypertext documents. Navigation bars at the top, bottom, or side of a web page, with buttons that link to the main sections, can help the user to keep in mind the structure and content of the site. The use of frames can be another powerful feature that aids in navigation. Frames allow the computer screen to be broken up into sections, or sub-screens. A horizontally or vertically divided screen, for example, can offer navigation options that remain constantly in view as the site is explored, with new selected content appearing in the body or main screen. This not only facilitates navigation, but it further helps to maintain a consistent design or style throughout the site. Even hypertext that resides on a different server can be configured to appear in the main screen as if it were part of the same site, a practice known as framing that can raise ethical questions about intellectual property rights. The use of invisible tables, like frames, is another web device that can be used to keep navigation options in front of the user. One column or row, for example, can be dedicated to navigation buttons or text, with the main body cells of the table left free to display the main content.

Computer-generated icons as navigation aids have similarly proved to be both popular and effective in web site creation. Computer users, by definition at the present time the vast majority of those who are accessing the web, have grown used to icons to represent different functions on their 'desktop' (itself a metaphor for the computer operating system). Thus, we click an icon of a printer to print a document, an icon of a disk to save a document, scissors to cut, and so on. It is therefore an easy transition to click an envelope to e-mail someone, a shopping basket to add products or items to a list for on-line purchase, or an icon of a little house to return to the Home page.

Iconography as a visual language that serves as a digital communications tool is an area that needs to be explored further. The effective use of icons can help in the communication and dissemination of hypertext documents to non-native English-speaking or English reading users. Icons take up less space than words and when used creatively and artistically, they can add suggested meaning and nuances to links by acting as visual metaphors. On the other hand, the overuse of clip-art icons that are freely available leads to tired, visual clichés that are best avoided. But at the same time, the custom creation of a set of obscure or esoteric icons that need to be learned by each new visitor to the site adds extra demands on the user; indeed the requirement to learn a new visual navigational vocabulary unique to a single site can sometimes only lead to further confusion and frustration. More research needs to be carried out to understand how we comprehend icons in order to facilitate the creation of non-linguistic visual aids that can be truly and intuitively understood.

For sites that are complex and contain large amounts of text and data, one of the most powerful features of hypertext is that search engines can be set up to locate and access content by key words, subject, date or any other criteria. Search engines can be configured to search only the existing web site they reside in, or else they may be set up to search the whole World Wide Web. They are very powerful tools unique to the hypertext publishing environment, but again, the content provider needs to ask whether or not it is of benefit to offer this feature.

Towards intelligent hypertext

A further problem with navigating hypertext documents is not simply the risk of getting lost, but also of not being able to find one's way back to material or a site that has previously been accessed. There are usually no intelligent associative links between the links themselves, and following one or another can lead the user further away from the original quest.

Long before hypertext and the World Wide Web were reality, in the years following the Second World War, an original thinker named Vannevar Bush, writing in the July 1945 issue of *The Atlantic Monthly*,[7] conceived of a mechanical device he called a Memex in which a user would store all his books, records and communications, and which would have the unique capacity, based on human memory as a model, to create threads of association, or 'trails of interest' between them. The technology that would enable this to take place was to be based on microphotography combined with compression techniques that anticipate our digital world today. It was a remarkable and prescient concept indeed, especially considering that this was a pre-electronic era long before the creation of the personal computer or CD-Rom, let alone the World Wide Web. Of course, the web does allow the user to retrace one's trails of interest or enthusiasms by means of Bookmarks, a personal aid to navigation that is the prerogative of each user. But Bookmarks simply record places visited, and do not draw associations between one site and another. Bush's system, by contrast, envisaged the creation of trails of interest all linked and cross-linked to one another by association, a considerably more powerful concept.

Indeed, to even begin to approach this vision, what may be needed now is a means of creating intelligent hypertext that can make such associations using the human memory as a model. Argue M.R. Kibby and J.T. Mays:

> 'We are doubtful whether the present exclusively manual methods for creating the links between elements of hypertext will prove to be viable.

Such links are more restrictive than the keywords used in many computer-based bibliographies; they present barriers to the exploration of hyperspace and are cumbersome to introduce and to manage even in small systems. They will become a limiting factor, ultimately to be rejected, in generating large hypertext systems ... for the same reasons that unstructured programming has been rejected by the computing community.'[8]

What is required, it would seem, is the development of some effective method of automatically generating links between hypertext documents based on both conceptual connectivity and/or semantic proximity, in other words, dynamically generated hyperlinks, perhaps created by robot search engines able to trawl the Internet on our behalf in search of connectivity.

It is clear, certainly, that the hyperlink, one of the most powerful features of content on the web, could be even more powerful still. What about links that are bi-directional, that is which point not only to associated material, but also indicate who is doing the pointing (i.e. who has linked to a specific site)? Once such a two-way, or indeed multi-way link could be established, then it could be possible for material to be shared between associated, linked sites, allowing an exchange of data between the two. Material updated on one site could automatically be pushed to all sites linked to that site. Or material on one site could be pulled into another site to bring associated texts together or to update content locally.

XML (Extensible Markup Language), though not yet fully implemented, is a meta-language that seems likely to be able to bring about such evolutions in hypertext and the hyperlink. By providing an in-built framework for meta-information, that is information and data about information, to be processed both manually and automatically, there is considerable potential in the future for the dynamic evolution of hypertext. Indeed the linking capabilities of XML already promise to be far more powerful than those of HTML, and should allow the management of such bi-directional and multi-way links. The possible impact of these and other developments that XML promises to bring to the entire form and shape of content on the web is considerable and it will be fascinating to see how hypertext evolves as a result.

The implementation of the next generation of web browsers combined with any further developments in HTML and the eventual full implementation of XML (which will not replace HTML but rather work above it on another level) will certainly result in the evolution of dynamic hypertext that depends less on the fixed or static, manually-generated link. Changes are happening fast, but what seems fairly certain is that hypertext itself, however it evolves and changes in years to come, has now established itself as a form of mainstream content, a form virtually unheard of only a handful of years ago, and is here to stay. The challenge for content creators remains to grasp and understand the form as it continues to evolve dynamically both now and in the future in order to be able to create compelling and effective content for the web.

1 J Conklin, 1987, 'Hypertext: an introduction and survey', *IEEE Computer 20* (9), pp. 17-41

2 Elizabeth Duncan, 1993, 'A faceted approach to hypertext?', *Hypertext Theory into Practice*, ed. Ray McAleese, Intellect Books, Exeter, pp. 133.

3 It is worth pointing out, however, that each search engine and directory has its own means of finding and cataloguing sites: some utilise metatags, others catalogue content on the Welcome or Index page. It is essential that a site is registered carefully with each of the target directories to ensure that the listing actually appears. If you don't want to do this by hand, a laborious and time consuming task, then there are companies which specialise in such tasks. Two examples are Web Promote at http://www.WebPromote.com/ and Submit It! at http://www.submit-it.com/

4 Deborah M. Edwards and Lynda Hardman, 1993, 'Lost in hyperspace', *Hypertext Theory into Practice*, ed. Ray McAleese, Intellect Books, Exeter, pp. 91.

5 *Ibid.* p. 104.

6 Lesley Allinson and Nick Hammond, 1993, 'Glasgow online', *Hypertext Theory into Practice*, ed. Ray McAleese, Intellect Books, Exeter, pp. 68.

7 An electronic version of Bush's farsighted article 'As We May Think', first published in the July 1945 issue of *The Atlantic Monthly*, has been published on the web by Denys Duchier, University of Ottawa: http://www.isg.sfu.ca/~duchier/misc/vbush/

8 M.R. Kibby and J.T. Mays, 'Towards intelligent hypertext', *Hypertext Theory into Practice*, ed. Ray McAleese, Intellect Books, Exeter, pp. 139.

CHAPTER SEVEN

Writing for the Web

In spite of the latest generation of browsers that promise ever more audio and video, and of the graphics-led interfaces that currently feature prominently on today's most up-to-date web sites, this is still a medium that is essentially text-based, and looks likely to remain so for the forseeable future (which admittedly in this field is not very far). A picture, after all, on the web is worth often more than a thousand words; or to put it another way, the time and bandwidth necessary to deliver graphics (still pictures let alone memory-voracious animations and video) is still disappointingly disproportionate to that required to deliver straightforward text. The site that depends excessively on graphics and snazzy design effects, with scores of slow-loading images for text headlines and complicated image maps, is still likely to take more time loading than the average web user is willing to accept.

Make no mistake, good design has now become an essential part of the web. But the fundamental basis of the web, as we have already seen, is hypertext, in its essence a word-driven system. Hyperlinks remain mainly text-based (though it is of course possible to use images as links), and even the way that search engines pick up sites based on key words means that text is paramount to the functioning of the web. And yet, many who are responsible for creating web sites today lose sight of this essential fact. The seduction of the visual – of the screen or monitor full of bright colours, images, and flashy animations – means that in many cases, the driving forces behind much of today's web development remain within the design studio, while the text is added almost as an afterthought.

Within this overall process, where are today's writers? On the whole, I fear, lagging some way behind today's designers in terms of taking advantage of the opportunities presented by new media. As a writer myself, this strikes me as surprising. For this after all is a medium that has the wonderful capacity to empower all writers to become publishers. Why then do professional writers on the whole seem to be slow in taking advantage of this great opportunity? The barriers may be at once economical, technological, and mental.

The professional writer who self-publishes on the web may still find it near impossible to gain any significant income from this activity, and thus it remains perforce lower down on the list of priorities compared to other opportunities for professional work. And, in a world that seems ever more dominated by the visual image, many of the companies who are commissioning much new web work today may be more comfortable spending large sums of money on web design than on the creation of effective text that should be an equally important element of web content.

As far as the technological expertise required by writers to publish on the web, the barriers may be more imagined than actual, but they can seem very real indeed. The jump from typewriter to word processor was for most writers a fairly intuitive one, but even at that, the transition was not always painless. The need to master new skills to write and publish on the web may now be seen by many as an even deeper and more unbridgeable chasm. But any such fears should be allayed. It is not strictly essential to know HTML to write and publish on the web (there are many web editing software suites that can effectively generate the code in the background). A new generation of scanners and digital cameras, allied with intuitive graphics manipulation software created for new users not professional graphic designers, is making it easier than ever to prepare images for publication on the web. And the skills necessary to transfer files onto a remote server are minimal: the systems operator of a host server can usually provide a set of instructions that explains the process, which in effect is little different from transferring files across an internal local area network.

While it is not, then, at all difficult for writers (or anyone for that matter) to acquire the skills necessary to publish content on the web, nonetheless, I have found through carrying out workshops with writers that mental barriers also exist which keep many from exploring the possibilities of publishing on the web. Fear of material being stolen through perceived lack of copyright protection as well as fear of invasion of privacy are two common concerns. In other cases, aspiring writers worry that by self-publishing on the web, material will no longer be considered for 'first rights' by literary journals or magazines, an area that is by no means always clear (if in doubt, query your proposed publications before uploading material onto the web).

Opportunities for writers

It is worth weighing out such real concerns against the potential benefits and opportunities that can accrue to those writers who make the effort to master the skills necessary to publish on the web. For creative writers, the web provides a forum for an evergrowing opus of new writing, in some cases exciting experimental writing specially created for the medium. Indeed, interactive fiction, or hypertext fiction where readers can decide where they want a story to go, has emerged as a new form of writing. Traditional forms of content such as fiction and poetry are published extensively on the web, providing new writers with an audience, something which in many cases may be more valued than financial renumeration.

The web provides professional writers with new outlets for commercial work, both writing for electronic publishers, and commercial and corporate clients, as well as creating and publishing new content (and finding new models to make this economically viable, including advertising, sponsorship and hybrid publishing). Academic writers have been posting research and articles on the Internet long before the web was created. New and emerging electronic academic journals, which referee content thus granting it the same authority and prestige as in traditional printed journals, provide further outlets for academic publishing. Indeed the web presents the by no means insignificant possibility for articles, theses and dissertations to reach global audiences, rather than languish gathering dust, read by just a few individuals before being consigned to the virtual dustbin of the lower stacks of a university library. And of course, the web is a powerful self-promotional tool, allowing all writers to advertise their services and works, to publish existing work in order to reach a greater audience, as well as to publish new work created specifically for the web.

It seems certain that as the web evolves, and especially as it becomes accepted as a mainstream medium as common in the living room as the office, then opportunities for writers with basic web skills and know-how will only increase. Certainly, it is a medium too powerful for writers to ignore.

Creative hypertext

As the web is an entirely new medium, it is not surprising that new forms of creative and imaginative content are evolving which follow no known rules and attempt to push the medium towards its always expanding outer limits. Not all such works are remotely successful or high quality, but the types of imaginative content that are being produced demonstrate that this is a vigorous and energetic medium that positively encourages exploration and experimentation.

Concrete, visual and aural poetry

Concrete, visual and aural poetry utilise the multimedia capacities of the web, and explore the spatial characteristics of web space through the use of animated typography, integration of visual images with text, and the use of sound, including background sound effects as well as poets reading their own work. *After Emmett*,[1] for example, is a visual poem by Mikel And that consists of 53 screens each made up of a three-by-three grid of animated letters and punctuation marks. The animated typography creates a remarkable rhythm of patterns that is achieved through the creative combination of various typographic fonts that cause the letters to dance, sway, shrink or swell as if they were organic forms. The work is a tribute to Emmett Williams, one of the first concrete poets.

Another web site that publishes visual and sound poetry is UbuWeb[2]. Through the capacity of the web to deliver sound files, the particular aural resonance of poetry can be conveyed; for example, the site includes clips of poets reading their works (such as the Futuristic Italian poet Martinetti) by using streaming audio clips and the RealAudio plug-in. Scroll,[3] another avant-garde web site that encourages writings that push the medium to its fullest has published some innovative creative work. 'Lung',[4] for example, is a story/poem by Brenda Keesel with text, visuals and background sound effects. Though it requires the Shockwave plug-in, its dreamlike, sea-like quality is very effective and demonstrates how the medium is unique in bringing added qualities and dimensions to creative work through multimedia.

Interactive fiction

From the earliest experiments in hypertext, there have been attempts to create interactive fiction, with varying degrees of success. The principal concept is that the reader decides where a story should go. Options are given, thus allowing the reader to make such decisions, so in effect there are potentially numerous diverse story lines that can all intercept and which can result in different outcomes and movements. Not surprisingly, perhaps, some of the best examples of interactive fiction are found in formula genres such as suspense or murder mystery works[5] as well as fantasy and sci-fi. In many cases, the skills necessary to construct such interactive works are as much those of computer game programmer as they are of writer. The best can resemble some of the more thoughtful fantasy computer games, though usually by definition they depend more on text than visual effects.

The nature of interactive fiction, like that of hypertext of any genre, is essentially non-linear, so such stories or narratives may often be entered or exited by different doors; thus, they may have no real beginning or ending. This can be troubling to both reader and author. True interactive fiction, moreover, does not simply allow the reader to choose from pre-determined options. Many interactive stories actually invite the reader to contribute by continuing or creating different threads of a story. 'The Neverending Tale',[6] for example, is an educational experiment in communal hypertext writing, intended mainly for children.

On-line diaries

The emergence of the daily or near daily web diary is a fascinating new genre that demonstrates the immediate and intimate power of the medium. Indeed, there is a growing opus of such web diaries,[7] produced by individuals for any number of reasons, which provide a fascinating day-to-day record of life in our time. Individuals, of course, have long kept personal diaries, but the very nature of the diary has hitherto been essentially a private one. The web diary, by contrast, allows writers to bare their souls to a potentially global audience. Many such diaries, moreover, actually seek to discourage visits from people who know or are related to the author with warnings such as, 'If you know me, go away' (as if they would). The implication seems to be that people want or feel the need to express themselves no longer just privately but in a public forum, happy to let perfect strangers eavesdrop on their most intimate moments and thoughts, yet wary of those whom they care about peering in too closely.

Of course, the reason the web is such an ideal medium for quotidian musings is the sheer ease by which material once composed can, at virtually the touch of a few keys and buttons, be published live immediately onto the web. Since many individuals who hold dial-up Internet access accounts are routinely offered free web space for their own personal use, the cost of doing so is virtually negligible. Thus, that daily journal entry, written in a basic word processing software, a web editor, or directly into HTML code, can be most easily and quickly transferred from private computer to public network simply by uploading the page or pages to the individual's private web space. Indeed, the rise of the on-line diary is another example of how the new medium, with its potential for immediacy and intimacy, has resulted in a creative new genre of content.

Traditional fiction and poetry: the PDF option
While new media creative content specifically composed for publication on the web is an emerging new genre, this is a medium that can also serve to deliver traditional creative content – short stories, poetry, even full-length novels – most effectively. For example, authors might not care to alter existing works to optimise them for the new media and the demands of the electronic reader, but prefer to deliver them instead in their original, unchanged format: the words remain the same, it is only the method of delivery that differs.

Therefore such works can most easily be published in HTML format on the web, though writers should consider how they wish their work to be accessed. For, as already mentioned, thoughtful text such as poetry and fiction may not be best appreciated when read on-screen. HTML files, on the other hand, may be difficult to optimise for printing and reading off-line (it is hard to control line spacing, typography, margins, and page layout in HTML).

In such cases where an author considers that a text or content is more suited to being read off-line, then consideration should be given to delivering such works not in HTML but rather utilising Adobe Acrobat's PDF[8] (Portable Document Format). By 'distilling' an existing document (it can be a complicated page-layout or a simple word processed document) into PDF, an electronic near facsimile of the printed document is created that can be delivered over the web, and accessed by users who have Adobe Acrobat's freely available Acrobat Reader software. Such documents can then be printed out in exactly the form intended by the author, to be subsequently read from hard-copy off-line.

Creating PDFs from existing text files is a simple enough process (far simpler than converting a document or text to HTML). The resulting PDF files can be uploaded on to and retrieved over the World Wide Web, they can be sent out as e-mail attachment files, or they can be distributed on CD-Rom or other transportable media (floppy or Zip disks). The PDF files, importantly, can be accessed across almost all computer platforms by all those who have the Adobe Acrobat Reader. However, though this software is widely distributed and freely available, this requirement may still prove to be a barrier for widescale universal access.

The tools of the trade

What is needed to publish on the web? Of course I've already assumed that you have access to a reasonable personal computer. No great memory or hard disk requirements are necessary to create HTML web content, though if you envisage doing considerable amounts of image manipulation, then you will need to ensure that your hardware is up to scratch. You will also need a modem, ISDN modem, cable modem or other device to connect to the Internet, thus enabling the transfer and retrieval of files of digital information. For adding images, you may also wish to invest in a flatbed scanner (a machine that captures both visual images or text and translates it into digital form), a film scanner (a similar machine that is able to translate and capture either negative or positive, black/white or colour film into digital images), and/or a digital camera. It is also necessary to have software for manipulating your images, as well as optimising them for publication on the web, a process that generally involves, among many other things, reducing colours in order to get image file sizes down to an acceptable size.

Is it strictly necessary to learn HTML in order to publish on the web? Yes and no is the short answer. As I've said, the use of Adobe Acrobat and PDF allows material to be made 'webbable' without learning a single line of code, and indeed PDF is a highly useful format above all for texts that are best printed and read off-line. But HTML still remains the common language upon which the World Wide Web is based.

Undoubtedly the generating of HTML code by hand is a tedious and time consuming task and quite frankly, for many it would seem to be an unnecessary distraction from the principal job of creating content. Fortunately there are now many powerful web editors and site creation tools available that perform this task in the background, leaving the content creator free to concentrate on composing, writing and creating designed text, rather than getting bogged down in the minutiae of what is, admittedly an arcane and confusing looking code.

On the other hand, while the latest versions of web editing suites attempt to support the latest features currently available on the web, they inevitably soon go out of date, simply because new elements and features are extending the functionality of HTML all the time as the markup language evolves. Therefore a software package that is sufficient today may well be deemed not powerful enough for your needs in six months time, and it can be difficult to keep up with upgrades. There will come a time, inevitably, when you feel that you must simply roll up your sleeves, open up the source code of document, and tweak the HTML commands yourself in order to gain greater control over layout and positioning of elements, typography, or any number of other elements.

This is by no means as difficult as it looks and for anybody serious about publishing on the web, I strongly urge you to make the effort and at least familiarise yourself with the elements of HTML. By studying a good handbook, this can be picked up in a day or two to a reasonable degree of proficiency. Not only is a working knowledge of HTML useful for content creation, it also enables the content creator to view other web pages and, by looking at the HTML source code (available in Netscape by the command 'View Page Source' and in Internet Explorer by 'View Source') to see exactly how someone else's pages have been put together. This can be a hugely valuable resource indeed.

Now, provided that you have space available on an Internet host (many Internet Service Providers or ISPs provide free space, while there is no shortage of companies offering web space for rent), you simply need to be able to upload, that is transfer your pages of HTML code as well as your images and other digital files (sound, video, whatever) on to the server. Once done, these pages will be immediately accessible to a potential global audience through their own particular URL, or Uniform Resource Locator, the address for each particular web site. There are various ways to transfer files from computer to the web. The simplest means is by FTP or File Transfer Protocol. Using FTP software, this simply involves gaining access to your Internet host by means of a username and password, then transferring files from your computer to the host server.

There are, of course, many more elements that relate to web production that demand considerably advanced and further skills: java and javascript, CGI scripting using complex computer languages like C++ and Perl, and much else. There are furthermore software tools that the web content creator can use to help analyse visitors to a web site, thus allowing you to gain a precise picture of who your audience is and where they are coming from. Such skills may be more advanced, and in any case, the web author who needs them may choose instead to farm out such services to freelancers. The point that this chapter makes is that simply by mastering the above basics, you can quickly and easily upload material on to the web that is immediately accessible by users anywhere in the world.

The rhetoric of hypertext

Every form of writing is an exercise in rhetoric, of persuading the reader to trust and believe and be interested in the content on offer. The style and approach to creating web content naturally depends on the type of content that is being presented. Certainly the way that substantive, detailed information is presented persuasively on the web, as in any other media, is a craft, the approach to which depends on a number of factors, most particularly, what is the main purpose of the publication and who is the target audience? The answers to these questions will, to a great degree, have considerable bearing on how content is constructed, organized and presented.

The style and tone of language that one chooses to employ is likely to be different if the audience is mainly teenagers than if you are addressing senior citizens. If the function of a web site is mainly to entertain through the presentation of provocative or avant-garde content, then the organisation and approach is likely to be different than the web site that aims to present factual information in a logical and clear manner. The web site that presents academic content is likely to be organised differently than the web site that serves to sell or promote a product. The choice of language in a literary site will almost by definition be different than that employed in a site that highlights pop culture. And of course the text that is intended to be read on-line is likely to organise and present its information in a manner that is quite different to that of a document that is meant to be accessed, printed out, then read off-line.

Writing for the web, moreover, has its own unique rhetorical devices. The use of hyperlinks, for example, effects the overall visual impression of a web document, the bits of coloured text adding credibility and suggesting further avenues of exploration, thus adding depth and authority to the document. The invitation for the reader to interact with the content creator or author is another rhetorical device unique to this medium; it suggests that content is fluid and organic, quite the opposite in fact, to content set in permanent type or print, and subtly suggests the potential for intimate interactive dialogue with the author. And further rhetorical devices such as visual clues, icons, and typographic effects are utilised to aid in navigation, and allow the author some degree of control over where the user is likely to visit.

While content may either be produced especially for publication on the web, or repurposed from existing text for the web, there are certain basic rules or suggestions that relate to effective hypertext construction. Some of the most fundamental findings from web usability studies[10] are that web users do not actually read on the web; rather they tend to scan material quickly, picking out the most important and relevant points before moving on elsewhere. Furthermore, users do not like long pages that require excessive scrolling; preferred text, by contrast, is short, concise and to the point. And finally, given that there is so much hyped content on the web, users trust information that is presented calmly and factually, void of marketese, jargon, or the hyped, 'hardsell' presentation of material.

It is, of course, important that any decisions relating to approach, style, tone, organisation, and presentation of a web site are ultimately made depending on each web site's overall requirements, function and audience. Nonetheless, the web has been around sufficiently long for some basic principles for the construction of effective hypertext to be offered. That is not to say that every web site author will wish to follow these guidelines as if they were carved in stone: think of them instead as set in impermanent electronic digital hypertext, literally here today, perhaps gone tomorrow, but worth for the moment, at least considering.

Know your audience

Think long and hard about who your target audience is. Present your material in a form and language that makes it accessible and understandable to this audience. Think of your audience's requirements: why have they come to this web site?; what do they need or want to know?; how can you get them to bookmark the site and come back? And give consideration to what level of technical expertise, hardware and software levels your audience is likely to have. If you know that your audience is grossly non-technical, for example, you will need to keep your design and content structured to a low common denominator to ensure that it is accessible, for example, to users with older, low level browsers, probably accessing the web through slow modem connections.

Organisation of material is critical

Before beginning the construction of a web site, it is critical to organise your ideas in a logical fashion so that as content is created, you know what and how the various hypertext documents will link together, both to each other as well as to other external hypertext documents. Create an outline of the site with main sections set up as separate directories or folders and use a visual aid to assist in this process, producing, for example, a flat plan map of the site that visually demonstrates how files link with each other, and where external links go to.

Give thought at this early stage as to how users will navigate a site. What directories or indexes need to be present at all times; should the site be set up using frames or tables to assist in navigation?; can users who enter from various portals figure out where they are? Effective organisation of material is essential for any web site to be successful.

Conceive content in chunks

Hypertext demands the organisation of material in self-contained, non-linear chunks. Such an approach may require considerable reorganisation of existing linear material in order to organise it effectively for the web. Sections should develop single ideas or points – related or tangential ideas are best highlighted through links, but be careful about inviting your reader to click elsewhere, especially to external links, too early.

Remember that users may access material in any order, so it may be essential that such sections are able to stand on their own. Sections should not be overly long – two and a half screens is generally considered about the maximum – as users find it difficult and tiresome to access information that requires excessive scrolling.

Text should be written clearly and concisely

A good hypertext document, like any good document, demands that information is presented clearly and in a jargon-free manner that is understandable. The need for clear, concisely written text that avoids long or complex syntax or complicated vocabulary is even more pressing in a medium where users scan rather than read word for word, and where it is critical that information is delivered and accessed quickly. Since the web is a new medium, it seems that simple, informal language works best rather than literary or overblown formal styles of writing.

Keep paragraphs short and to the point

The paragraph remains the unit of composition on the web as on the printed page, the grammatical container that represents a self-contained thought, argument or chunk of information. Keep paragraphs short and to the point, with no more than one main argument per paragraph. Readers are used to the convention of the indented paragraph, so use indents, as in print, to separate paragraphs, rather than non-indented breaks with line spaces or separation of ideas with horizontal rules. Since text is often scanned rather than read word for word, ideas are best organised from the top down, with the most important points presented first, and any amplifying information following.

'Page' length

Remember that the length of a web 'page' depends on the end user's screen size: a page developed and tested on a 17 inch monitor at 1152 x 870 pixels resolution, for example, will look considerably different to that same page viewed on a 14 inch monitor at 640 x 480 pixels resolution: the former, quite simply, will display a larger area, potentially wider and deeper than the smaller monitor. So if you want to make an immediate impact, ensure that your content will fit on a single screen window in the browsers that you consider your target audience will be using (the entry level for new PCs is now 15 inch monitors). On the other hand, if you have lengthy text or content, then accept that users will simply have to scroll down to access it. How small can pages be? If a succinct nugget of information needs to be offered, then a web page can be just a single paragraph or image. However, always ensure that the requisite navigational furniture is included on each page to ensure that visitors can find their way to the other sections of the site.

Use headings, sub-headings and lists

As users prefer to scan text in the first instance rather than read dense chunks of text on-screen, it is important that the main points of a hypertext document are clearly made to stand out through the use of hierarchical headings and sub-headings. The use of style sheets can be one way to assist in organising such headings and sub-headings logically and consistently. Lists are also effective means to help summarise main options or points in a hypertext document. If text is lengthy, or broken into lots of sub-sections, then consider, if appropriate, adding a brief table of contents at the top of a page, linked to the sub-sections by anchor tags to help the user find his/her way around (anchors are usually internal hyperlinks which when clicked take the reader to a particular section of a document).

Use typography creatively to change the beat and keep a user's attention

In order to achieve interesting typographical effects that you know will be displayed on most user's browsers, type must be rendered as non-editable image files. Such files, though adding considerably to the file size of a document, can be effective in presenting headings (use of shadowed type, embossed type, etc.), initial drop capital letters, animated type, navigation buttons, and other such effects. When combined with javascripts, for example, type can be made to appear to change colours when a mouse cursor passes over it (by swapping images 'on mouseover').

Typographical design features such as pulled quotes, a device that glossy magazines and newspapers often use, can be effective in a web site. Pulled quotes highlight in larger or bold text a statement that stands out from the rest of a text and can help to draw attention to the most relevant or important points.

Help the user to navigate a site

Use visual clues such as navigation bars and icons to help the users find their way around a site. Consider using tables or frames in order to present such navigational information consistently and permanently on a site, with, for example, links to the main sections of a site on a top navigation bar, and links to sub-sections within a left-hand column navigation section. Furthermore, there is a convention that textual links to a site's main sections may be offered at the bottom of each web page in small type. It seems prudent, indeed, to adopt such a 'belt-and-braces' approach where web navigation is concerned, and at the risk of being repetitive, to offer as many links to main and other sections from a variety of options as you can. In that way, you can at least minimise the risk of visitors getting hopelessly lost within your site.

Use abstracts or summaries to present lengthy material

If lengthy chunks of text need to be offered, then provide the user with an abstract or summary. This should be written concisely and to the point, clearly outlining what to expect in the full article, main sections and sub-sections, which of course should all be interconnected through hyperlinks and anchors.

Hyperlinks add credibility and authority to a hypertext document.

Hyperlinks also bring a web document alive and add depth and authority to a hypertext document. Use them wisely and considerately. Some prefer that links are gathered together at the end of a hyperdocument rather like a collection of footnotes in order not to distract from a considered reading of the text;[11] but most web authors feel that a hypertext document is in essence a structured document that should contain as many coloured or underlined links as possible to invite the reader to explore more deeply elsewhere.

Links, if textual rather than graphic, should be created from significant or meaningful words and phrases and they ought to be placed within a contextual framework that helps the user to know where he will be taken (unless you are offering links serendipitously, inviting the user to go on a journey of discovery that leads to somewhere not anticipated). Always consider whether links offered are truly necessary: too many links can be counterproductive, inviting users to exit your site and visit elsewhere.

Make your document interactive

Hypertext has the unique capacity for content creator and user to interact and establish a dialogue. Make use of this powerful feature by including a guestbook, questionnaire, or at the least by offering an e-mail facility so that readers can contact you. Getting users to interact positively is a first step in engaging your visitors to enter into the unique community that your site represents.

Security and privacy

It is so easy to publish on the web that it is quite possible unwittingly to present information or content that, in retrospect, you may not actually want the world at large to have access to. Therefore, think and think again before publishing any private or corporate information that is potentially sensitive. Even when placed behind limited distribution areas of a web site, robot search engines may be able to regularly search and index such material.

Also reassure your readers of *their* privacy and rights. If you invite them to sign a guestbook, don't ever use or pass their names on to third parties without express written permission.

Editing and publishing

Creating content for the web, no matter what the form or nature of that content, this chapter has argued, requires on the part of the writer an entirely new approach to the conceptualisation, organisation, research, and actual construction of language. The publication of web content, just like the publication of traditional printed material, furthermore requires the consideration of a number of other elements in order to be successful. In the case of print, the traditional workflow is that a writer delivers a text or manuscript to the publisher, who then hands it over to the copy-editing, design and production teams. The copy editor's task is to ensure that the text is well-written and free of errors, and furthermore that it conforms to that publisher's house style, marking up different levels of headings and sub-headings and sometimes working with the designer to bring textual, typographical and visual elements together. The editorial and design teams then work with the production team, making last minute corrections to proofs or, at the final stage even ozalids, while the designer meanwhile checks colour proofs, layouts and pagination, and undertakes such specialist tasks as colour corrections.

In the emerging work methodologies that relate to web publishing, the writer may similarly be one single element within a larger production team, working with designer and webmaster (who may sometimes be the new media equivalent of a project editor or editorial director). In such cases, the writer may supply his text, get paid, and leave it to the others to put the whole together. More than likely, however, the writer may be required to undertake additional roles and tasks in the effective creation and distribution of content on the web. Indeed, I have stressed throughout this book that the web offers the writer the opportunity to be a publisher, that in effect the writer need no longer be dependent on the services of outside editorial, design and production specialists to produce and distribute our work. On the other hand, this makes it inherent that the writer who publishes on the web masters and undertakes some of the roles and tasks traditionally undertaken by others.

Copy-editing

Precisely because the web makes it so very easy to publish instantly, it is also now never easier to publish sloppy and error strewn work. By contrast, the act of putting words to print, like that of carving them literally in stone, has always entailed a certain unspoken commitment to their permanency, to their importance. The very effort involved in producing a book, magazine, or even in-house brochure, not to mention the production costs, has always entailed that considerable effort is devoted to eliminating errors, factual, grammatical, and typographical or mechanical. I still remember well the days when an author received so-called galley proofs, long sheets of undesigned text, the first stage of seeing typescript transformed into typeset print. With galleys, sent to editor as well as author, the author had a relative degree of freedom to make even fairly substantial changes. Then followed first page and sometimes second page proofs. By the time the latter came around, the work had been, or should have been, gone over with a fairly fine toothed comb, and it was imperative that only the most necessary changes were carried out at this stage since it entailed considerable addition to production costs – the addition of a sentence or even just a few words could entail changes to pagination.

Today even in the world of print, such thoughtful stages, once part of a book's production cycle, may no longer be carried out. The technology now exists in theory to go direct from author's disk to printer's plate, and as exciting as this prospect is, it inevitably means that some of the basic editorial tasks and intermediate and final stages of proofing will be lost, to the possible detriment of the finished work.

Similarly, it is easy when publishing on the web to overlook some of the basic tasks that are, or at least should be, part of any editorial project. Many of the same rules apply to publishing on the web as to publishing in print, yet it is disappointing how often they seem to be disregarded. Perhaps because the medium is so new, and because it represents such a different approach to publishing, content creators and publishers alike often seem more than happy to let poorly written copy find its way on to the web.

Most web editing programs may have spell checking programs which ought to be used as a matter of habit (though check to make sure the dictionary is English, American or whatever your requirements). Text furthermore needs to be copy-edited not simply to ensure that it is well written and free of errors, but also to ensure that it is structured most effectively for the web, bearing in mind some of the suggestions given above. And attention should be given to such typographic design matters as consistency of type size, typeface, headings and sub-headings.

Editing web site content, furthermore, entails more than simply editing the body copy. Because each web document is an HTML document, it is equally important to ensure that the HTML as well as any additional javascripts or other such material is correct and working on your chosen browser platform. If you become proficient at writing pure HTML then you can probably edit the source code yourself, but most will wish to use an HTML validator, either on a web text editor (such as BBEdit for Mac users), or by running the HTML through an automatic checker on the web itself.[12]

Since a hypertext document, by its very nature, is linked to other hypertext documents, it is essential to check all internal and external links to ensure that they are functioning correctly. These are all part of the web copy editor's tasks.

Design, navigation and overall appearance
It is essential to remember that the actual appearance of your web site as it is seen by the end user will inevitably remain to a great extent outside of your control. Users' preferences relating to typefaces, type sizes, spacing, colour of links, whether or not they are underlined, even whether or not images are displayed, and many other such variables (the hardware configuration of the users' system, whether mouse or keyboard driven, monitor size, etc.) means that all your careful design work might well count for little or nothing. One of the great benefits of HTML is its capacity to distribute material regardless of computer platform and system requirements and it is thus at its heart since conception a content-, not appearance-oriented format. There is little the content creator can do about this except beware of the pitfalls.

Notably, it is especially important to test a web site in different browser versions. Netscape and Internet Explorer, at the time of writing, may have virtually cornered the browser market, but there are still many people using early versions of both. Netscape 1.0 and 2.0 and early versions of Internet Explorer do not support java or javascript, for example. Tables often display differently. Background colours may not be supported. Some tags are not supported in early versions such as those used to centre text.

If you only test on the latest browser versions, or those that you yourself use, then you won't really have any idea of how the same material will appear on many other browsers and computers. Mosaic, Lynx, Opera and other alternative browsers are still in use, while new browsers for hand-held appliances are appearing or set to appear in the very near future. It's not just the browser software that has an impact on web appearance, either. PCs may render colours and default type altogether differently than Apple Macintosh computers.

The content creator and editor must be aware of such factors and try to conceptualise how a site will look in different configurations and set ups. Web TV will furthermore result in users sitting considerably further away from the screen than from a computer monitor. So the caveat is, always test on different browsers and platforms, then test again and again. And always give consideration to your various users' requirements and expectations, now and in the future.

Add meta-information to a hypertext document

It is important that the writer of a hypertext document is equally aware that a number of invisible text elements need to be added to a web site, especially to assist the user in locating a site as well as to assist robot search engines in finding and cataloging a site and its collection of documents.

Every document, for example, needs to have a title, as indicated by the <TITLE> tag element. Such titles, furthermore, ought to be absolute, not relative to a web site. When a browser such as Netscape or Internet Explorer displays a hypertext document, the title of that document appears at the top bar of the browser window; if the user bookmarks that document for future reference, it is stored under this title name. It is important therefore to choose titles that accurately reflect and if possible summarise the contents of the page. Subsequent page titles in a web site should be absolute not relative so that in instances where users choose to bookmark a page, the title will be comprehensible (for example 'Teotihuacan Ceramics index' rather than simply 'Index' or even 'Ceramics index').

Some search directories utilise the opening text on a web site's Index or Welcome page to extract key words and site description. Many, however, depend on the invisible <META> tags that sit at the top of a HTML document so before registering, it is essential to give considerable thought to these tags. Particular attention therefore needs to be given to the following, inserting your own particular content within the "":

<META NAME="KEYWORDS" CONTENT= "">

<META NAME="DESCRIPTION" CONTENT= "">

Choose keywords with care, considering how potential visitors to your site might find you if using a search engine (what keywords they would type in?), and include all possibilities. Different <META> tag key word content and descriptions should be used for each different page or section of a web site, if relevant.

Register with search engines – helping users to find your site
One of the most important production tasks in web site creation is registration with search engines and directories. This must be done systematically so that the site you so painstakingly and carefully created can be found by any and all who are interested in it. It is essential therefore to devote considerable attention to registering with the principal search directories and robot search engines. The actual task of registering sites with these useful and highly visited site directories[13] can be a laborious and time consuming one. There are services that will undertake registration and site submission for you, though in my experience, it may still be best to go through the main directories one by one, manually following their particular requirements and procedures and selecting the most precise categories that are most relevant to your needs.

Before registering with a search directory, therefore, it is always worth spending some time exploring how that directory is organised. Try it out, check out sites that are similar in content to yours, see which categories and sub-directories they come under, and give considerable thought to your description, keywords, and, perhaps most important of all, from where or how a user is likely to search for a site such as yours. Then, only once you have a clear strategy for attracting users (and have included the <META> tags in your site as outlined above), register manually with each of the main directories. And remember, once you have registered a site, it may not be easy to change your entry, so it is worth getting it right the first time.

In addition to registering with search directories, there are a number of What's New announcement pages to whom you should submit your site, as well as numerous web awards. In order to be considered, it is merely necessary to spend some time checking out those which are most relevant to your content and then informing them of your site's URL.

Another way to promote your web site is to subscribe to relevant newsgroups or e-mail discussion lists; become an active member of these communities, include your signature together with your web site URL on any postings, and whenever relevant, point people to pages on your site that may contain information that is of use to them. And of course, don't forget to include your web site URL address on all printed material, including letterheads, visiting cards, bills.

Give credit; don't plagiarise

No writer in any medium, it goes without saying, should ever consider stealing material from others or using or quoting material without giving it due credit. There seems to be something about the web, however, indeed about the very nature of hypertext documents, that positively encourages, what shall we say, the sharing of material between one another.

On the web, there can be fine lines between linking and plagiarising. The use of frames in particular can cause problems wherein material created by others can be opened within a new window and presented in such a convincing manner as to seem part of a different site altogether. Honesty and integrity are as important on the web as they are in traditional publishing and pirates who steal others' copyright material for their own use or profit should rightly be regarded as the parasites of the industry. If you are offering extensive links to other sites, always make clear what you are doing and where you are coming from, and above all give credit where it is due.

Acceptable content

For those who believe in freedom of speech on the web, then naturally there are certain obligations imposed on the responsible content creator to ensure that that which is published is acceptable within the broadest confines of decency. Unspoken codes of conduct have emerged, and are emerging still. The Internet in its earliest days was strictly non-commercial, for example, and though the web has changed all that, most newsgroups still consider the posting of blatant commercial messages, a practice known as 'spamming', to be unacceptable.

Naturally the definition of what is acceptable and unacceptable regarding web content varies considerably from individual to individual. But as human beings, surely we ought to inhabit some common moral ground. Certainly there is a great deal of gratuitous obscenity and pornography on the web, but so is there in the real world. Where the web is at its most dangerous is not simply as the purveyor of offensive material, but rather, much more dangerously, through its interactive and community-building capacities, those same powers which we elsewhere applaud as a powerful feature of the new medium. Thus, those obscene sites and user groups that encourage the creation of communities that revel and traffic in paedophilia and the sharing of child pornography must be universally shunned, I imagine, by most decent human beings. Similarly, those web sites that serve as an active and literal call to arms for extremists, racists, bigots, terrorists, football hooligans and the like are abusing the power of the medium for unacceptable ends.

It is sometimes hard to draw the line as to what is acceptable and what is not. On the one hand, we may applaud the use of the web as a medium for rallying support for freedom fighters. But what about its use by those sectors or sections of society whose beliefs and values we don't share? Right wing militia, criminals, child abusers, bigots and racists, anti-western fundamentalist terrorists? Is it fair to celebrate the power of the medium only when we agree with what it is being used for?

The right to freedom of expression and the control over the dissemination of dangerous and unacceptable content are difficult issues that we as content creators and users of the web must consider deeply, searching our own consciences as we grope to find a middle way that does the least harm.

Maintenance

The nature of interactive web publishing means that once you have uploaded your site, that may be only the beginning. For the web is not and never will be a medium where content is carved in stone, left for years, months, even weeks unchanged. It is most powerful as a timely, up-to-date medium that reflects the changing world we live in. It is worth bearing this in mind before embarking on a web project in order to be aware that considerable time needs to be set aside for regular maintenance.

Update regularly

If you want to get people to make return visits, and indeed to bookmark your site, then it is essential to keep it up-to-date by changing and adding new content as frequently as necessary. How frequently you change your content naturally depends on a number of factors, above all whether you have new and compelling content to add. There is no point ever in adding superfluous or unfinished content simply to put on something new. It is a good idea, however, to have a clear strategy at the outset for updating so that your users will know what to expect. Quarterly updates are the least frequent that I would suggest; monthly or weekly updates might be more useful for your site; and in some cases, topical information, or an on-line diary for example, might necessitate daily or near daily updates. Always point out new material on your Welcome page (a 'New' button or logo can be used), and consider including a date at the bottom of a page which indicates when it has last been updated.

A web site that includes frequent updates may need to include some sort of archive for past material. If this archive is likely to grow into a vast database of searchable and useful information, then thought should be given to including an index and perhaps even a search engine to help users access it.

Check your links and check again

It is essential to check from time to time all external links that you include in a site. Such pages can move; they can be updated in such a manner that they are no longer relevant to the relationships or contextual associations that you are drawing; they may become so popular that they are difficult to access and thus give repeated 'error' messages; or they can disappear completely. So even once your site is up and running successfully, as part of your regular maintenance program, you should systematically check such links periodically.

Analyse who is visiting your site

Unlike most traditional print media, the web has in-built powerful mechanisms that enable the content provider to learn a great deal about the audience that visits your site or sites. For indeed, all those who come to a site may leave considerable information about themselves that is recorded in that site's unique log. The intelligent interpretation and analysis of such information[14] can give you real clues about your audience: how many visitors you have received and on average how long they have stayed on your site; what countries, cities, or states they come from; even what hours of the day and days of the week are most popular. You can find out whether your audience mainly accesses your site from home or work; what browsers and versions of browsers they use; what are their favourite entry pages; from which page do they most usually exit your site. Moreover, it can be extremely useful to know what the top referring search engines and directories are; what key words are most often used in searches that lead to your site; and whether there are other sites that link or refer to your site. Such valuable information can help you to direct your site more effectively to your chosen audience, to tailor material to your users, and to make changes that will allow you to reach out to find new visitors.

Campaign to eliminate web litter

Another task that the content creator needs to give some attention to is the mundane job of housekeeping and the tidying up of web litter. Throughout this book, I've stressed the ease, speed, and minimal expense with which content can be published on the web. This means, however, that it is equally easy to upload test versions or drafts of material that may never be intended for general public viewing. Similarly, pages or whole sites may go out of date or simply become no more relevant than last month's newspaper. And yet, such material, even when uploaded as 'hidden' pages that are not registered or linked to any other pages, can cause considerable clutter: robot search engines relentlessly trawl the web in search of new material and may inadvertently register such pages. In other cases, pages that have been registered then moved or shut down, may still be listed on search directories, thus leading users in many cases up the virtual garden path.

Yet because web space is cheap, human time costly and limited, little attention is given to this ever-growing problem. It is easier simply to leave out-of-date material on a host server than it is to eliminate it. But the web is growing at such meteoric and exponential rate in any case that we risk being overwhelmed by new content as it is. Web litter – inconsequential or out-of-date content – only compounds the situation.

It is therefore good web practice to clean up after ourselves. Do your bit for the cyber-environment by using FTP or telnet to delete any such obsolete files or directories.

1 Mikel And, 'After Emmett': http://net22.com/qazingulaza/joglars/
afteremmett/bonvoyage.html
2 UbuWeb: http://www.ubu.com/
3 Scroll: http://www.behaviour.com/scroll/toc/
4 Brenda Keesel, 'Lung' on the Scroll web site:
http://www.behaviour.com/scroll/story/l_story/l_story.html
5 Some examples are catalogued on the Yahoo directory:
http://www.yahoo.com/Recreation/Games/Internet_Games/Interactive_Web_Games/I
nteractive_Fiction/Mystery/
6 'The Neverending Tale': http://www.coder.com/creations/tale/
7 An interesting web ring of almost daily web diaries is Often:
http://www.ounce.com/often/
8 For more information about PDF, see the Adobe Systems web site:
http://www.adobe.com. The section devoted to Adobe Acrobat is
http://www.adobe.com/proindex/acrobat/main.html
9 Some popular and powerful web site design and creation tools, which add far more than HTML code and support advanced dynamic features such as java and

javascript, cascading stylesheets, and layers include Allaire HomeSite, Macromedia Dreamweaver, Net Objects Fusion, GoLive Cyberstudio, and HoTMetal Pro.

10 Fascinating and in-depth research into such issues has been undertaken by Jakob Nielson and John Morkes. See 'Concise, Scannable, and Objective: How to Write for the Web': http://www.useit.com/papers/webwriting/ writing.html

11 The web edition of the *The New York Times* adopts such an approach in its on-line articles, with hyperlinks within an article anchored to main external links given separately at the foot of the article. http://www.nytimes.com/

12 There are a number of validation sites that will allow you to type in a URL and receive a page of HTML errors line by line. The definitive HTML validation service is offered by the W3C: http://validator.w3.org/

13 Such as Yahoo!, Alta Vista, Lycos, Magellan, Metacrawler, and many others.

14 There are various ways that log stats can be analysed. Some service providers may supply an intelligent analysis of the log. Alternatively, software is available that enables you to extract the raw log statistics from your host then interpret it in an intelligent, graphical fashion. WebTrends is one firm that offers such software: http://www.WebTrends.com

CHAPTER EIGHT

Virtual Communities

The web's most potent and as yet still underrated facility, possibly, is its capacity to relate, interrelate and bring together information from disparate sources located on remote servers anywhere in the world. A single document no longer exists on its own but can become part of a greater whole that is constantly being added to, revised and amended. Such content which goes beyond the single document creates in the process virtual communities of interest that are literally held together by no more than the invisible electronic web that binds them.

By its very nature as a many-to-many publishing medium, the web would seem to have an in-built mechanism for creating communities. TV, music, newspapers, and books can create communities, too. Witness the conventions of 'trekkies' who have for decades now taken on Star Trek personalities and re-enacted episodes at conventions around the world; the so-called Deadheads who, in following the rock band Grateful Dead, felt themselves to be part of an alternative anti-establishment sub-culture; the communities formed by fans of books by Tolkien and C.S. Lewis, Dickens and Trollope; and even just the sense of camaraderie and shared values that we feel with those who read the same newspapers as us.

An essential difference, however, may be that the web's community building power grants those with shared interests and values a voice and a means of active and immediate participation, all from the armchair comfort of our own computers or web TVs. This is where the web's synergetic power, at once publishing medium and communication medium, comes to the fore. For the content creator, this means that tools such as e-mail, the use of discussion lists and forums, and live communication by means of Internet Relay Chat (IRC) allow not only the creator and user to enter into a dialogue, but for the users themselves to strike up relationships and discussions between themselves, irregardless of the content creator. Thus, any web site has the potential to form an active and involved community of interested individuals, and for that community to exist, thrive, grow and evolve in ways that the content creator himself may never even have envisaged or, once released, be able to control. Indeed, for the content creator there is something at once both exhilarating as well as frightening about this prospect!

A broadly accepted definition of the term 'community' is a group of people either living in the same locality, or having common interests or shared beliefs. A real life community may have its centre where members meet for social, cultural or recreational purposes; or else, its sense of communion may not be dependent on physical or direct social intercourse. Indeed, in many cases, members may belong to a community, but not necessarily share a sense of communion, of belonging. I've been a member of many sports clubs in order to make use of facilities, but have often not felt one iota in common with other members. Scientists or academics who belong to a select community based on common interest may sometimes feel not communion with other members but perhaps even antipathy if not direct competition. We are all members of a number of communities at various and usually simultaneous moments in our lives, based on work, family, our children's schools, sport and other recreational interests, or religion and beliefs, yet many of these communities may never overlap, and we enter into them only when circumstances or need arises. In other cases, our membership of a particular community may define who and what we are and indeed give us our very identities.

A virtual community can serve many of the same functions of a real community, but the main difference is that social interaction and communication takes place primarily or exclusively over computer networks linked by telecommunications networks. In the process, this brings people together from various places and walks of life and disparate geographical areas who might not be able otherwise to do so. Members of virtual communities may eventually go on to meet in real life (sometimes with unpredictable or even dangerous results), but this is not necessary for such an electronic community to thrive and prosper and evolve. Indeed, it seems, perhaps curiously, that poised on the knife edge of a new millenium, we are more than happy to enter into such invisible communities, form personal interrelationships with total strangers, indeed to trust, care about and nurture such relationships which in the process can become as real – as vital, as infuriating, as meaningful – as any that we have in the physical world.

The power of virtual communities
A virtual community may be simply a web ring of individuals who share an interest in, say, the poetry of Emily Dickinson, the inner workings of the stationary engine, or good parenting; it may be freely open to anyone and everyone who cares to drop by, or it can be closed, a members-only venue defined by vocation, special interest, the payment of a subscription, or any number of other delimiters; its members may be mainly passive 'lurkers' or it

may have a core of active and involved individuals, all feeding bright ideas off one another, helping to solve communal problems; and in number, it may have just a handful of members yet still be vital and worthwhile, or else it may have members in the hundreds or even thousands.

Virtual communities exist for no other reason than to bring like-minded people together – without that *raison d'être* of common interest, they quite simply would wither and die, or never even form in the first place. Real life communities, by contrast, are often created by chance circumstance, for example, for no other reason than that people find themselves brought together physically by where they live, work, study, or play. People in virtual communities, though, are usually there by choice, because they actively want to be. They can thus be in a position to bring a commitment and energy to the virtual community that is sometimes lacking in real communities. Moreover, the invisibility of the virtual community means that its overriding common interest remains foremost even to the exclusion of obvious and otherwise distracting differences. It doesn't matter (and no one need know) where you live in the world, whether you are male or female, black, white or yellow, physically or mentally able or disabled, or whether you are 14 or 84. Your credibility and place in a virtual community is based entirely on your own desire to be involved, your participation and contribution to the community, as well as your authority in terms of relating to that common shared interest that is the focus of each particular community. In this sense, virtual communities are often far more democratic, fair and unbiased than communities in the real world.

A virtual community can bring together by electronic means a shared pool of expertise and knowledge that is in many cases unsurpassed. It seems a fact of life that people who have amassed considerable knowledge and expertise in a particular subject may very well be keen to share that knowledge and expertise, often for no other reason than because they have the ability to do so. Certainly there can be great satisfaction in helping others by offering suggestions and advice; this inevitably confers prestige, authority and kudos on the giver, and this simple reward for such virtual altruism seems to be sufficient for many who participate actively in such communities.

Take an example. In the course of undertaking research recently for this book, I became a member of a virtual community concerned with a particular aspect of electronic publishing, Adobe Acrobat's PDF file format. The community functions through the medium of an unmoderated e-mail discussion list. This is freely open to all, a self-help problem solving forum for anyone who is interested in the topic. Not only did I learn a great deal from other members of the list about the topics and issues that it concerned itself with, it was furthermore extremely interesting to experience at first hand how this particular virtual community functions. It attracts many newcomers who have specific problems that they need help with, and it is remarkable how generous members with expertise always are in offering detailed practical solutions. A core of dedicated professionals are the most active, and no query, however elementary or seemingly obvious, has ever, in the time that I have been a member, been disparaged or dismissed as irrelevant.

Certainly, those who have consistently been most helpful have emerged as the main players of the group, and have taken on the unofficial status of leaders of the community, in the process gaining the respect and admiration of their peers. When particular questions are posed on the e-mail discussion list, I look forward with interest to see what certain members' points of view will be. Each may have their own voice, language and approach. On the other hand, when questions not at all relevant to the community are posted, thus breaking the unwritten rules of the community, the immediate replies, often penned by this same self-designated group of experts, can be scathing in the extreme in their scorn and sarcasm.

This is but one example of how such a virtual community can draw from a collective pool of expertise and knowledge, and directly assist in communal problem solving. In an active virtual community, very quickly an invaluable archive of postings builds up, and this can usually be searched and accessed, thus creating in the process an evolving, organic database of knowledge on a special interest topic that can become invaluable. This is a pattern that is repeated in virtual communities brought together for virtually any subject that you think of under the sun.

The benefits for those who contribute? Often no more, no less than a feeling of having contributed, of having added their own perspective and knowledge and point of view for others to see and use. Indeed, for communities to grow, it seems important that members have something actively to do, as well as something that they care about. In the process, a less tangible benefit of virtual communities, like real world communities, is that they have the capacity to give individuals a sense of belonging, something which should by no means be underestimated. In a world where people can feel increasingly isolated and alone, the ability of the web to reach out and connect people is a valuable one indeed, and if they can in turn feel that they are not just takers but contributors, too, then the potential for community building is immense. For those living in remote parts of the world, for individuals who live in populace cities yet still feel unattached and alienated, for the disabled, for the ill or housebound, and simply for those whose shared interests may be reciprocated only by other equally empassioned individuals not next door or even in the same country but rather on the other side of the world, the inherent power of the web to create such virtual communities is a very real and potent one indeed.

The dangers of community

On the other hand, the technology that enables such positive and helpful virtual communities to be created, can just as easily be turned in anti-social ways, too. In cyberspace, as in the real world, there may be as many bad communities as good ones. Much negative publicity has been given in recent months to the perverts and especially paedophiles who have created virtual communities for the dissemination of child pornography, even for the exchange of information about and the contacting of children through on-line services.[1] Other anti-social elements, notably seditionists, right wing militia, racist and terrorist groups, have similarly not been slow to make use of such technologies to form their own virtual communities.

Of course it can be argued that such anti-social communities exist in the real world, too. However, a very real danger of virtual communities is the sheer facility for anyone to find and join such communities. Indeed, the potential for abuse is great, for such communities can quite easily attract the young, impressionable, even through direct solicitation by e-mail. Information about members of legitimate communities may quite easily pass into the hands of the unscrupulous, and before you know what is happening, you or even your children could begin to receive communications from less than desirable communities. The issue of privacy and community is indeed a pressing one that needs to be addressed and considered by all who make use of new media: for the information, the trust that we place in virtual communities, the friendships and confidences that we have been so free to give (often to total strangers) within the confines of a select private community may without our knowledge and consent become available to a much wider public. And do we really want people to know about our most secret and inner feelings and desires? From the lonely and secret confines of our own private space to the global public of cyberspace – and all the weirdos lurking in it – may be but a too hasty mouse click away.

The web, it has already been noted, has a further in-built capacity to deceive. This is where, after all, people recreate themselves in their own imagined or desired images far more readily than may ever be possible in the real world, changing sex and sexual preference, personality, looks, even total identity. Such virtual deceptions can be carried over into real life sometimes with disturbing results. There have been instances of deceptions between individuals who have fallen in love with fictitious cyber-personae who have turned out in real life to be already married, or a different sex, age, or any number of other such deceptions. The feelings of betrayal tinged with profound disappointment can only be compounded by the disappointment of apparent sharing of trust engendered by the intimacy of the medium.

There are further dangers, too, when fantasy worlds, created and inhabited in cyberspace, collide with real life. In particular, there have been reported instances where fantasy acts of cybersex have led to real cases of attempted rape, actual rape, sexual abuse, stalking, even murder. Correspondence and private and public e-mails have been cited as evidence to corroborate provocation in the legal cases that have resulted.

Skilled imposters, conmen, rogues, liars, and charlatans certainly existed long before the creation of virtual communities. But the message seems to be that virtual communities may be particularly ripe for infiltration by them, not least because we seem to be less at guard, more trusting of words typed across our screens by total strangers than by words spoken to our faces in the real world. Could it be that the intimacy of the written word allied with immediate telecommunications over electronic networks encourages this often blind trust? This is certainly a phenomenon worthy of further investigation.

The virtual community as commodity

Virtual communities by definition bring together groups of focused individuals with shared and common interests. In the process, community originators, perhaps even unwittingly, may suddenly find themselves with something of significant value: the community as commodity. For indeed, sponsors, advertisers, commercial concerns, academic, profit and non-profit organisations may be attracted by nothing more than the ability to reach out and communicate to the focused collection of individuals which a virtual community brings together.

Indeed, some of the biggest players in the web world have not been slow to realise the value of creating such communities. Thus, in recent months, a new buzzword in the concept of web development is that of 'portals' or gateways to web content. Companies such as Yahoo! (with its My Yahoo! offering), Excite, Netscape (with its Netcenter), Microsoft and others are aiming to attract users to their sites by offering them free services such as customised news, free e-mail accounts, even web space. The catch? By getting individuals to enter the web through their particular site, they can deliver potentially millions of 'eyeballs' to advertisers and sponsors. Indeed, as the mechanism for gathering information about users becomes ever more sophisticated, focused banner ads can appear on users' screens for topics or products that they have previously expressed interest in. Or else when a user enters a search directory portal to find out about something, then cross-referenced advertisements may appear together with the search results.

Are the millions who sign up to such gateways, though, really members of true communities even in a virtual sense? Perhaps not. But what about those services which aim precisely at creating special interest communities. The Globe is one such example. Members who choose to subscribe can select those environments or virtual spaces where they feel most at home: arts & entertainment, infobahn, life, globe, metro, romance, or special interests. Members are furthermore provided with free e-mail, as well as with the tools for creating both members' profiles (which can be surprisingly revealing) as well as their own Home pages. In this manner, the Globe provides a vehicle for the creation of any number of special interest virtual communities, from those keen on music or the arts, to communities of singles, pet lovers, or people living in a particular region or city. There are forums for live chat between special interest group members as well as e-mail discussion group forums where members can post communal messages for others to read and respond to.

Geocities is another successful example of a web site that consists of a community of communities. Members, similarly, are offered free e-mail and web space, and they are furthermore invited to join 'neighbourhoods' that reflect their special interests or enthusiasms. Some Geocities neighbourhoods include Napa Valley (food, wine, dining out, the gourmet lifestyle), Enchanted Forest ('a neighbourhood for and by kids'), Bourbon Street (jazz, cajun food, southern culture), Vienna (classical music, opera, ballet), Soho (art, poetry, prose, the bohemian lifestyle), among many others. The keyword here seems to be 'lifestyle': Geocities is inviting individuals to identify themselves by joining specific virtual communities, and to go further by creating content that adds value to these communities through the granting of free web space. Indeed, in this fashion, the members themselves have been enlisted, quite willingly and free of charge, to create content, a more than valuable commodity.

Such commercial community building web sites serve a useful purpose: they give individuals a place where they can reside in cyberspace, comfortable among others with like-minded interests. Furthermore, such individuals are granted the tools to express themselves, even the free web space in which to do it. Meanwhile, for advertisers and sponsors, certainly, the grouping of individuals into such neat categories, and the consequent potential to reach focused, targeted groups is immense.

On the other hand, the groupings of individuals in this manner can be somewhat contrived and artificial. In many ways, more valuable virtual communities may emerge from the grassroots. Witness the scores of e-zines, electronic publications which like their low-budget paper equivalents, fanzines, are produced by individuals not driven by commercial concerns but by their enthusiasm and sometimes fanatical passions for their subjects. Indeed, it is in this area of the web that often the most compelling content is found. And it can be in such areas that the most dynamic and vital communities form naturally and unselfconsciously, by discussing, arguing, sharing information passionately and sometimes vehemently, above all because the members of that community care deeply about their topic, whatever it is.

Creating virtual communities

The choice of subject matter for a web site is the first step towards defining its potential community. The web is particularly powerful in bringing together special interest or niche groups through specialist web sites, often created by those who are already enthusiastic members of such groups. Indeed, though the web is often cited as a medium that can reach upwards of 100 million potential users, it is perhaps at its most powerful in its ability to bring together 50 or 500 or 5000 individuals who care passionately about some narrow and specific topic. The prospect for niche or boutique special interest community building on the web is unlimited.

Like the creation of any content, the choice of design, style, and language are the means by which the content creator consciously defines a target audience and potential community. A web site with a sober, hierarchical structure on a grey background and with limited images and graphic content may address primarily a serious academic community; a design-led web site requiring the latest third-party plug-ins in order to function, on the other hand, may limit that site's potential community to web savvy professionals, the only ones who keep up to date with the latest technologies; a games arcade approach to design, by contrast, combined with 'groovy' language and humour can attract a youthful community. The point is that at the earliest stages of the conception of a web project, thought ought to be given to the potential audience and of how to attract that audience into becoming not just one-off visitors but commited members of a vital and worthwhile virtual community that forms around your site.

E-mail, the 'guestbook', and interactive forms

Simply by placing a contact e-mail address on a web site grants it community building powers. E-mail should by no means be underestimated by the content creator for it enables the establishment of an immediate interactive dialogue, allowing the visitor to a site to communicate with the creator, and for the creator to communicate with the visitor. This can be a private one-to-one dialogue – a visitor fires off an e-mail or completes an interactive form or questionnaire to the content creator giving feedback about the site, or striking up a dialogue that continues for a number of e-mails – or it can be a public posting in the form of a guestbook.

A guestbook invites a comment or posting which will be read not only by the content creator but by any who care to peruse this section of the site. A guestbook is usually driven by a CGI (Common Gateway Interface) script that resides in the CGI bin or directory on a web site's host server. When a guestbook entry is filled in, and the Submit or Send button is clicked, this causes the information to be sent to the script, which instructs the fields of the message to be displayed on a separate web page, usually together with all the previous guestbook postings arranged by chronological order.

Similarly, some web sites, in return for providing further or supplementary information, ask visitors to fill in a questionnaire or survey in order to learn more about them. Such forms may also be driven by a CGI script which delivers the completed form to the content creator in a format that can be analysed intelligently.

The use of such scripts adds interactive power to a web site, and though the scripts themselves can seem daunting to set up, there are considerable resources on the web which can assist in the process.[2] Indeed, there are many such scripts that can be copied and used for free, and require no more than minor modifications before being uploaded onto a web server using the normal FTP protocol, though getting the script to run correctly on your particular web host may require support from your Internet service provider's help desk.

When gathering information from your visitors about themselves, it is polite to ask whether or not they mind receiving further mailings, electronic press releases, and the like. I certainly would not consider it ethical ever to pass on or sell this information to third parties, or at the very least only if you have their written permission to do so. Also, if you hold personal data on individuals and groups of individuals on your computer or web server, you may be required to register with your country's equivalent of the UK's Data Protection Registrar.[3]

Newsletters and electronic press releases

Inviting your visitors to take part in a dialogue by e-mail is only the first step towards creating an effective and vital virtual community centred on your web site. It is equally important to engage their attention and to continually bring new and refreshed content to the fore. Once you have a database holding the e-mail addresses of interested visitors who have taken the time to e-mail you, sign your guestbook or complete an on-line questionnaire or form, then you can consider bringing your web site to their continued attention through the use of an electronic newsletter. If you choose to create an electronic newsletter, it is best that it is sent out on a regular basis, so give due consideration as to how and who will generate the material, how much time will need to be set aside for this task, and whether there will be sufficient worthwhile content that can be generated on a regular basis to warrant such an investment.

It is always a good idea to allow visitors actively to choose whether or not to receive such regular information. It may be offered on a 'push' basis only to those who actively choose to subscribe; or else, in the first instance, you may choose to send an electronic newsletter to everyone on your database, explaining why you sent it to them, and indicating that if they do not want to receive further issues, then they can easily unsubscribe, for example, by hitting the Reply button and sending a return message with UNSUBSCRIBE in the subject box. By this manner, not only do you not find yourself in the invidious position of being a 'spammer', i.e. someone who sends out unwanted or junk e-mail, furthermore, you know that you are posting your newsletter only to those parties who are actually interested in receiving it, a first and vital step towards creating a virtual community of interested individuals.

An electronic newsletter not only serves as a vehicle for timely, updated content, it furthermore keeps your web site to the fore, and serves as a regular reminder for interested visitors to return to it again. Like those who subscribe to a regular daily newspaper, it serves actively to engender a sense of community, of belonging, to those who are privileged to receive it. But to be successful, like any publication, it needs to have content that is of real interest to your chosen community. This does not mean simply corporate or marketing content, but rather content that informs and/or entertains, and offers material of real and genuine use that would otherwise not be available.

Electronic press releases can serve a similar purpose, and may be more suitable to annouce both special events or one-off news items.

E-mail discussion lists and newsgroups
Once you can get your visitors talking not only to you, but to each other, then a virtual community can really take off and begin to have a life of its own. One way to achieve this is through the setting up of a moderated or unmoderated e-mail group discussion list.[4] Members subscribe to receive all the postings to a particular list, and in this way correspondence takes place in a semi-public forum that is sent to all the members of that list. If someone needs particular advice or help with solving a problem, for example, then that e-mail request can

be posted, it will be received by all members on the list, and anyone on the list can choose to answer or offer suggestions. Should members wish to correspond in private with other members, especially about matters not relevant to the list as a whole, then they can choose to do so. In cases where a list generates a lot of traffic, that is, dozens or more messages a day, then there may be a mechanism whereby members can subscribe to receive a digest only of the list, that is, a single e-mail containing a brief summary of each day's postings.

If the creator of the list so chooses, then a list can be moderated, that is, all messages are filtered through a moderator who either edits them, or deletes messages that are deemed either not relevant or unsuitable for publication (for whatever reason or criteria decided by the moderator or the list members as a whole). Moderated lists may be more focused, and include fewer items that are irrelevant to the list as a whole then unmoderated e-mail discussion lists; but on the other hand, they may inevitably betray the bias of the moderator, something that may or may not be a good thing. Sometimes the best virtual communities are those that are allowed to flourish and develop in their own direction, with as little control or imposition of values or central point of view as possible. Others though might value the editorial focus that a good moderator can bring.

Newsgroups are another way of creating virtual communities. Newsgroups can be created on virtually any topic, provided there is sufficient interest to form and maintain a group. Like e-mail discussion lists, they consist of communal messages between members of a list which are available for all to read. Outsiders can enter the discussion, too, for unlike e-mail discussion lists that are sent out to members who have chosen to subscribe and have that day's e-mails sent to them, newsgroups can be accessed by anyone interested in a particular subject. If you post a message to a newsgroup, you have to go back to check that newsgroup's 'message board' to see if you have had a reply. Archives of the newsgroup list are usually available, and you can choose how far back, i.e. how many messages, you choose to download at a time. Most newsgroups utilise tools that enable related messages to be 'threaded' or grouped together, that is, responses to a newsgroup posting are grouped with the original message in order to keep topics comprehensible.

Newsgroups are organised into categories and sub-categories. Alt. for example is short for alternative and may include the most offbeat groups. Biz. is for business related newsgroups, while Rec. is for any type of hobby, sport or recreation. There may furthermore be strict etiquette for participating in newsgroups. The most fundamental caveat is that with the exception of business categories, they should be strictly non-commercial. The practice of posting commercial messages, the equivalent of electronic junk mail, is strictly frowned upon, and if you inadvertently partake in this activity, then you are more than likely to be 'flamed' – that is receive a tirade of angry, sometimes personally abusive insults.

Live chat

Correspondence by e-mail or newsgroup, whether one-to-one or through a group discussion list or newsgroup, is asynchronous, that is, the messages are sent and replies come inevitably with a time lag that can be the result of both the delay in a message being sent and delivered across the Internet, as well as through the delay that it takes people to access their e-mail, read and think about such messages on- or off-line, then compose and send their replies. Though still incredibly immediate when compared to the days or weeks' time lag that was inherent in letters sent and delivered by the postal service (now dubbed 'snail mail' by web users to distinguish it from speedy e-mail), nonetheless, this asynchronous medium of communication is far less immediate than, say, direct speech either in person or over the telephone.

However, the technology now exists whereby web sites can include live chat rooms where members or visitors can hang out and 'talk' (by sending keyboard messages) directly to one another in synchronous mode, that is, immediately, the words appearing on the receivers' screens almost as they are tapped into the keyboard, the immediate replies, made up on the fly as it were, creating a new form of informal, casual, sometimes dynamically charged electronic banter. Such conversations may be directed to any and all who are in a chat room at any one time, or they can be sent privately to individuals within the room.

In the past year, politicians such as Tony Blair, Britain's Prime Minister, have undertaken live question and answer sessions directly with the public utilising this medium; sports and show business personalities have met their fans and entered into direct communication with them; and scores of individuals for any variety of motives, routinely enter into chat rooms to meet old and new friends, carry on conversations or embark on relationships that may become as important and vivid as any in the real world.

To enter a chat room, visitors may assign themselves a moniker, that is an assumed nickname that others will know them by; in many cases this allows an individual to assume a character that may or may not reflect who they are in real life. In the case of serious chat rooms where people are discussing serious concerns, individuals may all use their real names; in fantasy chat rooms, and especially in lonely hearts chat rooms where people are desperately seeking other people, gender switching and fantasy role playing is sometimes the name of the game.

Virtual reality

The rather flat one-dimensionality of the text-only world of most live chat rooms can leave much to the imagination, one of their great advantages. Yet text-only communication typed on to a computer screen undoubtedly lacks the richness and tonal nuances, the meaningful pauses and infinitely subtle inflections of human speech. There are many, therefore, who feel that by adding a spatial element to chat rooms in the form of three-dimensional virtual reality environments may be a way of adding to the immediacy and interactivity of the cyber-experience.

In a virtual reality live chat room, you may not only assign yourself a moniker, you can also create a morphed three-dimensional character or avatar[5] that represents you on-screen and has certain behaviour, traits, abilities and prowess. As you choose to move across a virtual reality environment by means of your mouse or keyboard, your other self, or avatar, may be seen to move across the communal screens of that virtual environment. Thus, you can choose where to go, who to stand next to, what obstacles to encounter and overcome. Though at present, such virtual worlds may be limited by current technology, nonetheless, the possibilities for creative game and fantasy role playing in such worlds is immense[6] and certainly hints at possibilities that will no doubt evolve and be developed in the future.

Indeed, when virtual communities based on three-dimensional spatial or architectural models can be created, allowing us to interact with other individuals in real time and virtual space, then gradually the distinctions between the relationships we have in the real world and those we enjoy in cyberspace may become ever more blurred and indistinct. Such virtual reality chat rooms can be used for professional conferencing purposes, for the sharing of scientific or academic discussions over electronic networks, for brainstorming sessions, for educational purposes – creating virtual historical worlds in which role playing is used to learn about events – as much as for recreational purposes.

The fragility of community

At the end of the day, though, it must be acknowledged that tools such as e-mail, guestbooks, group discussion lists, newsgroups, live chat rooms, and virtual reality environments are no more than that: just tools, albeit powerful ones, that can assist in the creation and nurturing of virtual communities. At times such communities may seem tenuous and artificial at best, but undoubtedly real and meaningful communities can be constructed by them which in time can come to exist, flourish, prosper, and grow, and all over electronic networks.

Yet such communities can also be as terribly fragile and vulnerable as any in the real world. As in any community, there is the constant need for the establishment of community values, indeed for rules and behaviour that are deemed acceptable by each community's members. Usually this is not something that can be imposed upon a community from the top down, but rather has to be allowed to grow and evolve organically, as interactions and behaviour within the context of a virtual community come to define what is acceptable and not acceptable, something that may well be different for each community.

Indeed, such community values go beyond the simplistic and unofficial 'netiquette' that is supposed to define on-line behaviour, but which in many cases only succeeds in the creation of a self-appointed élite. Each community must evolve in such a way that its ethics and values are apparent to other members. Obscene language may be acceptable and even encouraged in one community but totally taboo in another, its use resulting in that member being 'flamed' by other members to the point of exclusion (flaming can involve simply sending diatribal messages to the offending member or even such punishments as members sending communally huge numbers of e-mails to the offender's e-mail address, resulting in server crashes and potential mental breakdown). In other cases, unacceptable or disruptive behaviour, dishonesty and deception can in a very short time succeed in destroying the fragile and delicate sense of camaraderie, the very community that has been brought together. What is important, above all, is that communities' members know between themselves the rules – written or unwritten but explicit nonetheless – and that if they abuse them (by using members' e-mail addresses or information about them for marketing or commercial purposes, for example), then they will be banished or excluded from that community by electronic means.

Such values may differ considerably from those which we accept in the real world. For if in virtual communities we may be encouraged to recreate ourselves in our own desired image, adopt monikers and personae that are very different to how we are in real life, if we choose to partake in gender switching and cyber-adultery, then where is the fine line that separates acceptable and unacceptable deceptions? Yet even within the most offbeat and alternative virtual communities, there are likely to be boundaries beyond which it is not advisable or permissable to stray.

Undoubtedly the capacity to create and nurture virtual communities is one of the most powerful features of the web. Virtual communities, as indicated above, become valuable commodities; for sponsors, advertisers, commercial and non-commercial companies and organisations may like nothing more than to attract the attention of well-focused special interest groups, the so-called 'eyeballs of the web' so beloved of market analysts and web financiers.

It seems that while content creators can assist in the establishment of such virtual communities, not least through providing both virtual environments or space as well as the tools of construction, the best such communities may take on a life of their own beyond that originally envisaged by the content creator, and continue to grow and evolve organically in new and sometimes unexpected and surprising directions. Yet like anything organic, it remains the job of the content creator to ensure that the ground for such communities to grow in remains fertile and well watered, that any weeds and dead wood are ruthlessly torn out. Above all, it is important to create an environment where members of a virtual community gather not just out of self-interest (i.e. to get an answer to a question or a problem), but where they begin to respect, care about, and value each other's contributions. If such environments continue to be created and nurtured, then we can expect the growth of truly valid and worthwhile virtual communities to continue to luxuriate.

Some virtual communities

The Globe http://www.theglobe.com – provides free e-mail, events and live personality features, together with free web space as well as live chat forums for special interest communities.

Geocities http://www.geocities.com – members can choose from over 1000 'neighbourhoods' to hang out in.

The Palace http://www.thepalace.com – Over 1000 'palaces', that is virtual environments where 3D avatars interact with one another. As a member you can create and personalise your own avatar, and there is also software available for creation of your own 'palace' or virtual reality community.

Vroma http://vroma.rhodes. edu – a virtual community for the learning of classics modelled upon the ancient city of Rome. This is an imaginative and fascinating use of virtual community for educational purposes and the academic community.

The Well http://www.thewell.com – Howard Rheingold's original community is open to members by subscription only.

Bianca.com http://www.bianca.com – calls itself 'the alternative on-line community' and consists of 'shacks': members can create their own 'shacklets'.

Newsgroups

There are literally thousands of newsgroups on the Internet which can be accessed. They are organised into broad categories which are then further broken down into sub-categories. The following are some of the major groupings.

alt.   Probably the largest category of newsgroups – stands for alternative and covers diverse topics, from pop culture, music, sex, controversial issues.

biz.   Commercial category for business related newsgroups.

comp.   Computer hardware, software and systems newsgroups. Good place to find assistance on technical problems.

misc.   Miscellaneous groupings of diverse categories covering broad range of subjects.

rec.   Recreation, hobbies, sports, games, and cultural interests.

1 On 9 June 1998, the United States Congress unanimously passed a bill cracking down on paedophiles who use the Internet to entice children sexually, both making it easier to prosecute those who do so, as well as lengthening custodial sentences.
2 The CGI Collection, for example, has a number of free scripts that can be downloaded, as well as points the way to other CGI resources: http://www.itm.com/cgicollection/
3 The Data Protection Registrar http://www.dpr.gov.uk/
4 L-Soft is a company that can assist in setting up group e-mail discussion lists: http://www.lsoft.com/ Sparklist also provide group lists: http://wwwSparklist.com
5 The word comes from Hindu meaning the incarnation of a deity: the creation of avatars in virtual environments may allow us to extend beyond ourselves and even our computer screens in fantasy worlds, taking on whatever guise and personality that we wish to create.
6 At present, most true virtual reality environments need to be accessed by special VRML (Virtual Reality Modelling Language) browsers, which may either be stand-alone browsers or plug-ins that function within existing HTML browsers such as Netscape or Internet Explorer. An example of a rudimentary version of such virtual reality chat rooms, together with the software to achieve this, can be found at The Palace: http://www.thepalace.com

CHAPTER NINE

Design, Style and Content

Since Tim Berners-Lee created the World Wide Web, there has been a dichotomy between those who favour document structure over those more concerned with document presentation. This essential split between a structure-oriented and an appearance-oriented approach continues to a large extent today, since the very nature of HTML as a device-independent document markup language rather than a page description language self-imposes by definition considerable limitations on design, layout and style.

The subsequent evolution of HTML has, to a certain extent, reflected this concern as each new version of approvals to the markup language has gradually, in conjunction with the evolution of smart browsers, granted greater and greater control to the content creator to produce web pages with ever more complicated and precise design elements. The earliest browsers, for example, did not even support the use of images. The HTML code generated thus resulted in pages of text-based information, usually on grey backgrounds, with links underlined (for those viewing in black and white monitors) or in colour. Today's latest browsers, by contrast, support not only images, but furthermore tiled background images, imagemaps (designated sections of images that become hyperlinks), animated images, images that change when a mouse cursor rolls over them through the use of simple javascripts, even the limited use of video and sound. Tables and frames, meanwhile, assist in the layout and navigation of a site, while layers and style sheets help to ensure that the site envisaged by the content creator is as close as possible to what end users will see displayed at their end.

Yet in spite of all this, HTML remains a limited and inflexible language that allows only a single way to describe information and which is furthermore complicated by the scores of often incompatible proprietorial extensions that manufacturers have created in an attempt to extend its functionality. It is still therefore something of an exercise in jumping through hoops within hoops simply to get a page on the web to display even approximately as the content creator intends it to be. The roundabout ways of working with HTML that have needed to be devised even to achieve a modicum of control over the simplest layouts are complicated in the extreme – locking text into invisible tables nested within tables, for example, to ensure that columns or rows display correctly.

Particularly for designers who have grown up using desktop publishing tools (DTP) – brilliantly designed and intuitive software suites that really were a logical electronic development from the scissors-and-paste environment that preceded them – the inherent difficulties in creating web designs that the author or creator is confident will appear as intended (even more or less, let alone precisely) remain considerable.

XML (Extensible Markup Language),[1] an abbreviated version of SGML[2] (Standard Generalized Markup Language) will go some way to addressing these concerns when it eventually comes into full implementation, not least because it will enable a document's content and underlying structure to be separated from its appearance. This will, among other things, allow authors to be able to design their own document types tailored to the precise needs of a specific audience or community using custom markup elements and XML-specific style sheets (particular markup elements, for example, will be used by the mathematics communities in order to be able to display complex mathematical expressions and formulae, something at present very difficult in HTML; similar sub-sets of markup elements could be used by other scientific communities to meet their own specific requirements, or even by publishers wishing to display cookbook recipes through the creation of document type definitions). But even when fully implemented, it is not envisaged that XML will ever wholly replace HTML; rather, HTML, in a version adapted to be used within the XML environment, will continue to be used for the basic presentation and organisation of content and is therefore likely to be with us, in one form or another, for some time to come.

Design principles

Thus, even in spite of the promise that XML brings, a fundamental and essential design principle that must currently be accepted is that no matter how hard the content creator tries, the ultimate form in which web pages are displayed at the receiver's end remains to a large extent outside of control. Even when such basic elements as typeface, type colour, type size, and other such variables are written into HTML code, or even when they are embedded into a document as a style sheet, they can, and will be, overridden at many user's ends, for a variety of reasons. Some elements will be positioned differently. Colours may display differently from machine to machine (even within the same platform due to monitor variation) or even be absent altogether. Typeface and size defaults will be determined by the user not the content creator (to demonstrate what a radical difference user defaults can make, simply play around in the Preferences dialogue box of your own web browser with defaults for typeface and type size and colour, then look at a variety of web pages to see how they differ).

In web page design, therefore, it is essential to be flexible, allowing, indeed anticipating changes at the user's end in any variety of manners. With this approach, you may not know precisely how your pages are being displayed in any one place, but you can be fairly confident, having tested on different platforms and browsers, that they will not only appear acceptable but more importantly function correctly.

This book is not a primer in web design, and does not propose to suggest ways or tricks to jump through hoops or workarounds to achieve desired effects or special effects. Nor is it a tutorial in HTML. More in-depth books and web sites devote themselves specifically to these topics. Rather, the aim of this chapter is quite simply to offer some basic design principles and suggestions that address essential publishing concerns regardless of media – structure, organisation, readability – as well as concerns specific to the web publishing environment. For just as the transition from designing for print on computer utilising DTP tools required the development of new skills and awareness while at the same time maintaining many principles and working methodologies from the previous era, so does the transition of designing from print to the web require at once an awareness of new requirements yet a knowledge of basic design principles and methodologies.

Define purpose and potential target audience

Just as the purpose of a site and a target audience have an impact on the style of writing on a web site, so do they equally help to determine the overall approach to design, structure and navigation. If the purpose of a site is simply to present in-depth information to a specialist audience, then the design approach will be very different to that of the consumer web site that aims to entice and excite general viewers, with, perhaps, the ultimate aim of getting them to make a purchase on-line. A knowledge of the target audience, moreover, can help to define design parameters: is it a technically savvy audience that is probably using the latest browsers loaded with third-party plug-in applications like Flash, Shockwave, or Adobe Acrobat's PDFViewer? Or is it an audience whose knowledge and technical expertise is rudimentary or still developing at best?

Moreover, a decision needs to be made as to whether or not to design for the lowest common denominator – that is, say users on slow modem connections, using browser versions 1.0 or 2.0, viewed on 14 inch monitors at 640 x 480 pixels resolution – or whether instead to assume a fairly high level of software and hardware – say, newish PCs or Macs with sound cards, 15-17 inch monitors, fast modem connections, and the most recent browser versions.

Cascading Stylesheets (CSS)

One of the most significant developments in the evolution of HTML has been the adoption of the W3-approved specification for cascading stylesheets (CSS). This development in large measure reflects the need to be able to separate a document's structure from its display presentation. CSS enables a web site to have specified style attributes that apply to the whole web site, or individual web pages, specifying classes and properties, including typeface, type size, margins, leading, and much else. As such, CSS works in the same way as style sheets used in DTP and word processing programs. You can, for example, define a style for headings and sub-headings that includes typeface, size, leading, type colour, and other attributes and this can be applied throughout a web site. This means that it is far easier to make global changes to an entire site than was previously possible. Should a web designer wish to change one of the attributes, say, a typeface, this can be done simply by changing an external style sheet document that serves as a master set of styles for all other pages within that site.

CSS will go a long way towards granting web designers a modicum of the control that they have long enjoyed in the print environment. Therefore, they ought to be used by all web designers who care about how their web pages are displayed. That said, only the latest generation of browsers (Netscape 4.x and IE 4.x) fully support CSS, so consideration still needs to be given to workarounds required to achieve satisfactory results for the majority of users still on earlier browser versions. That said, the 'cascade' in the style sheets specification means that in theory it should be possible for a page to display satisfactorily in all browsers, at whatever level, as the specification allows for different specifications to be incorporated depending on browser and platform. In practice, this may involve considerable additional work, and results may still be unpredictable. Nonetheless, CSS is a significant development and should be supported.

XML style sheets promise to go even further. A entirely new Extensible Style Language (XSL) has been drafted to be used specifically within the XML environment. Based on formatting features in CSS as well as more powerful SGML standards, XSL will provide the syntax for the creation of an unlimited number of style sheets tailored to an infinite number of different document types. Standardised document type definition style sheets are already emerging for use on the web, a process that is likely to accelerate in months to come.

Design, structure and navigation

Because a web site by nature is a collection of hyperlinked documents, design is intrinsically linked to structure, and structure to navigation. Well thought out and produced design elements positively assist in creating and conveying a structure that is comprehensible, so consideration needs to be given to this at the earliest stages of a web site's formulation.

The use of horizontal or vertical frames, for example, which in effect break a screen up into separate screens and thus allow navigational elements to remain in place, with new content appearing in the main target window, can be powerful design elements that aid in structure and navigation. Invisible or visible tables, or even nested tables – that is tables within table cells – similarly can be powerful design elements to aid in structure and navigation. Other design elements that aid in navigation include menu bars, icons, buttons, and imagemaps (images with clickable hyperlinked hot spots). The creation of a set of visual graphic elements that can be applied throughout a site is one way of establishing a strong visual theme.

An important point to keep in mind is that each unique web design may in effect involve the creation or reinvention of a new user interface. The temptation in many design-led sites is to create a user interface that is clever in the extreme, something which has not been done or tried before in quite the same fashion. Herein lies the rub. Such an interface may inevitably require a steep learning curve on the part of the new user to master it: remembering what pictorial icons mean, figuring out a complicated structure, the use of imagemaps for links, or the requirement of first downloading a third party plug-in simply to get past the front door. The risk is that if you place undue demands on the user simply to master how to navigate or penetrate a site, then there is the real possibility that the user will click elsewhere and so move on.

Constant consideration needs therefore to be given to the imagined web user coming to a site for the first time. Is its structure and navigation clear and able to be mastered at a virtual glance? Does the design positively aid in navigation and help the user to find his/her way to whatever section or destination might be the desired goal? Are the rules established and followed consistently – an active link is coloured red, a visited link purple – so as not to confuse. Precisely because we do not yet have a complete set of protocols or rules that are universally comprehensible (some such rules have become established – a coloured bit of text usually indicates a hyperlink, for example), it is more important than ever to ensure that your unique user interface is above all comprehensible and consistent in order to be effective.

Design and maintenance

Consideration should also be given at the outset of a project to design and maintenance. How much maintenance will a site require, and does the design build in a mechanism for achieving this with the least effort? For example, what are the 'pages' that are likely to require the most updating, and can a template be made to allow this to be done easily at a later date? How about archiving material. Is there a structure in place that will allow this to be done easily and effectively? Again, the design and structure needs to be thought out carefully to incorporate such elements. For it should be remembered always that a web site, by its very nature, requires flexibility above all: one of the most powerful features of web publishing, indeed, is the capacity for content to be amended or updated on-the-fly, and the design needs to reflect this. Even the best looking site that is inflexible and incapable of being added to constantly without a great deal of additional effort or input will lead to problems in the future and possibly considerably extra work that would not otherwise be necessary.

'Page' size

The blank 'page' which the web designer starts with can vary in size considerably and this naturally has a large influence on design. Again, does one design for the lowest common denominator, that is, for a 14 inch monitor with a screen resolution of say 640 by 480 pixels? If that is the goal, then it is imperative that the overall page is no more than a maximum of 600 pixels in width. Vertical depth may be equally important. If you don't want the user to have to scroll down for content, especially for content arranged in multi-columns, then the maximum height should be no more than 400 pixels. In practice, this is a very limited area indeed, and though a screen can be scrolled both horizontally as well as vertically by means of scroll bars, it may be difficult to achieve both a satisfactory design as well as legible type for reading on-screen.

On the other hand, there is absolutely no point in designing a page that looks great on a 17 inch monitor and expecting it to achieve the same effect when viewed on a smaller screen. Again, it is necessary to view results on a variety of screens and resolutions, then arrive at a compromise result that is satisfactory.

Layout

In print, the grid is one of the most important means of defining the elements of a page in relation to each other and to the work as a whole. On first glance, web pages might seem to be free of the more rigid constraints and conventions of page architecture in, for example, printed books or magazines. Nonetheless some of the principles of good print design, especially in relation to the grid, transfer across to web design as well.

Layout on the web, for example, may be notoriously difficult to nail down precisely since so many variables are inevitably decided at the user's end. But within the looser and more flexible framework that this necessarily demands, the structure of a web page is often defined by a grid that contains a number of elements – navigation bars, vertical menu buttons, logos and page titles, hyperlinks, bottom-of-the-page end matter, margins, headings and sub-headings, single or multiple columns, boxed features, pulled quotes and much else. Other page furniture sometimes included on web pages are running heads (the title feature which appears in the web browser often serves this purpose), name of the author, date when last modified, volume or issue, index of hyperlinks mentioned in the body text, overall site map, and other such elements unique to the new medium.

So if web pages on first sight seem to be less rigid than their print counterparts, nonetheless a structural layout that incorporates the various and sometimes more complex components needs to be established which can be carried throughout the site (with scope for variations of course). The use of tables is one way to achieve this layout structure. By creating tables with absolute dimensions (given in pixels rather than as a percentage of the screen, which can vary from user to user), a flexible degree of control can be exerted over the positioning of these elements, though considerable hand 'tweaking' and checking and rechecking on different platforms and browser versions is still likely to be necessary.

Backgrounds, page colour and the use of white space

Early web pages tended to present type that extended across the full width of the screen, with no margins or white space, and often on dull grey backgrounds. Later manifestations of HTML supported the use of background images and many web sites now make use of coloured or textured backgrounds based on images that tile or repeat a pattern ad infinitum by using the <BODY background= " "> tag. Left-hand or right-hand borders can be created in this fashion to provide a background for navigational elements such as buttons or icons, while leaving the body of the 'page' blank, that is either white, solidly coloured, or with a light textured pattern. Alternatively, the colour of the page can be determined without the use of an image by specifying the required colour in the <BODY color= " "> tag. Black or dark page backgrounds with white or light coloured text are currently popular on the web.

If using either background images or a background colour, consideration needs to be given to two main factors: 1) on-screen legibility, and 2) printability. It is important to ensure that the type colour of both main text, as well as links and visited links are legible against the background or coloured background and this should be checked and tested in different browsers and platforms. Furthermore, it is important to give consideration to printability. Bear in mind, for example, that when using white type on a black or dark background, the type, when printed with background colours off may not show up.

Whether white or coloured backgrounds are chosen, it is as important on the web as it is in print to give consideration to the use of white space, that is, areas on the screen that are left blank. Particularly because reading on-screen can be fatiguing and difficult, it is important that web sites utilise white space to break up sections of long text. Margins in particular should be used, either by creating space through the use of tables, or by using the <BLOCKQUOTE> tag that causes text to indent from the edges of the 'page'.

Typography

As in other media, the principal role of typography is to be legible in order to get across a message. If typography can be pleasing and kind to the eye, and also add an element of style and design, then all the better. In print for magazines and books, typography can be at once tight and very carefully composed, since, viewed at arm's length, finer aspects such as kerning (letter spacing), and the avoidance of rivers (patterns of white space that appear in blocks of text) and widows (short lines at the top of a page) and orphans (one or two word lines at the end of a paragraph), can all be attended to.

The web places different demands on typography. Type that is intended to be read on-screen must above all be legible, and this is not always easy to achieve, especially given that it is not always possible for the designer or content creator to know how or what the user will see at his end. Because early versions of HTML did not allow typefaces to be specified, many web sites still leave such decisions to be decided at the user's end by default (that is, the default typeface specified in a user's system is what will appear). In many cases, this default is set at Times, an excellent typeface for print but one which is less successful for on-screen reading.

Screen fonts are based on a square pixel grid and are thus more legible for on-screen reading. There are increasingly a number of screen typefaces available and consideration should be given to choosing from these. Faces that are optimised for on-screen use tend to be more open, with wider letters and more generous letter spacing. Times is a fairly condensed face; part of its attraction for print was that it allowed more words per line and lines per page while retaining legibility. But on-screen, its tight letter spacing and crudely rendered serifs make it at best eye-fatiguing, at worst, in particular in small sizes, virtually illegible. Microsoft offers for free downloading a range of TrueType fonts developed for the web, including Arial, Verdana, Comic Sans MS, Monotype, Georgia, Times New Roman, Trebuchet, Impact and others.[3]

Later versions of HTML allowed content creators to specify typefaces using the <FONT> tag. The problem, of course, is that it is impossible to know what fonts may be available at a user's end. Mac users are likely to have one set of basic fonts, while PC users may have quite another. If a specified font is not available, then an alternative will be substituted. Therefore, the designs that you may produce on your Mac with typefaces available on your system may be likely to display differently on a user's PC with other typefaces available, and vice versa. Again, some sort of compromise is necessary to achieve required effects yet at a lowest common denominator that is acceptable.[4]

Mac typefaces	PC typefaces
Helvetica	Arial
Times	Times New Roman
Courier	Courier New
Symbol	Symbol
Geneva	MS Sans Serif
New York	MS Serif
Chicago	No equivalent
Zapf Dingbats	WingDings
Palatino	No equivalent

Normally, therefore, it is adviseable for a content creator to choose not a single typeface but rather families of typefaces, for example by specifying <FONT FACE= "Verdana, Arial, Helvetica, sans serif">. Thus, if the top level face, say Verdana, is not available on the user's system, then the browser defaults to the next specified, Arial, then to Helvetica, and finally to whatever generic sans serif face is on the user's system.

Type size is another area that needs to be carefully considered. Most web browsers have a default size of 12 point, but this can be increased or decreased by the user in his preferences panel. PCs generally default to a larger type size than Macs. In order to gain some control over the finished appearance of the page as well as on its legibility, it is wise therefore rather than depending on

either the default, or on relative type sizes – <FONT SIZE= "+1"> for example increases the font size up one size from the default – to instead specify a precise type size. But again, the difference in type size appearance varies considerably between typefaces, with a typeface like Times displaying considerably smaller than Georgia. For optimum on-screen reading, generally type should be displayed at either 12 point or 14 point depending on the face. Unless using CSS style sheets, this translates in HTML to <FONT SIZE= "3"> or <FONT SIZE= "4">. Though the latter may seem large for pages destined to be printed, the user can always choose to print at, say, 75 or 80 per cent. The smallest type sizes that are legible on screen are generally 7 to 9 point – <FONT SIZE= "1"> or <FONT SIZE= "2"> – though many typefaces do not render satisfactorily in these small sizes. Verdana or Arial, two sans serif faces, for example, render satisfactorily at 9 point, while Times is barely legible.

Using typography to give emphasis or priority to information

Typography is one of the ways that information can be emphasised or prioritised on the web, as on paper. This can be achieved in a number of ways.

Headings and sub-headings can be created using the <H> tag that creates text of different size in bold. You can specify requisite attributes of the heading in a CSS style sheet, too, defining, for example typeface, colour and size. Or else, headings can be created as in-line images whereby typography is created in a graphics application as a bitmap image.

Typographical style attributes can also be indicated using HTML tags. <EM> for example usually renders as italics, while <STRONG> causes type to be displayed as bold. But care and consideration should be given to using both these tags. Italics often appear not at all legible when rendered on screen (slanted type fights against the square pixel screen grid) while certain small typefaces in particular may be similarly difficult to read in bold.

Web sites often make use of coloured typography, both for body and headline text as well as for hyperlinks. In print, the use of coloured text is normally a luxury that is not usually considered due to expense. But on the web, it is as easy to add colour as to have text in black. Coloured text is most often used to designate hyperlinks. An early default convention that has become fairly widespread is that non-visited hyperlinks are displayed in red or blue type while visited hyperlinks are displayed in purple. User preference can also cause all such links to be underlined. But these colours and formatting can be overriden, and indeed they should be if these colours do not fit in with your scheme, background, or overall style and theme. Again, it is best, whenever possible, to attempt to impose some sort of definition and control over how elements display rather than leaving it to the user's default settings.

The use of typographical elements such as drop capitals is another way of adding emphasis. A drop capital can be created as an in-line image. Or a similar initial capital effect can be created simply by making an initial letter larger and in bold. Pulled quotes, that is, a section taken from the body text and blown up usually in bold, to be displayed either in a white space margin or in the middle of the body text, is another effective way of using typography to add emphasis. Pulled quotes may be positioned in tables nested within tables. The typographical effect of small caps can be achieved to give impact simply by varying the type size within the HTML code. For example the following code:

```
<FONT SIZE= "4">T</FONT><FONT SIZE= "3">HIS </FONT><FONT
SIZE= "4">I</FONT><FONT SIZE= "3">S </FONT><FONT SIZE=
"4">T</FONT><FONT SIZE= "3">HE </FONT><FONT SIZE=
"4">W</FONT><FONT SIZE= "3">AY </FONT><FONT SIZE=
"4">T</FONT><FONT SIZE= "3">ORLD </FONT><FONT SIZE=
"4">E</FONT><FONT SIZE= "3">NDS...</FONT>
```

will display as:

THIS IS THE WAY THE WORLD ENDS...

As in print, the positioning and orientation of type can be used to positive effect. Type can be positioned against the left-hand or right-hand screen edges, or it can be positioned centrally. In tables, vertical and horizontal alignment allow type to be positioned left, right, centre, top, middle, or bottom of table cells. If type is rendered as an image, then it can of course be positioned in any way at all, and interesting effects can be done with type, for example, running vertically up or down a margin of a page.

Measure and ratio

On screen, as in print, legibility is determined in great part not only by choice of typeface and type size but also by line length and leading, that is, the space between lines. In the earliest days of the web, type extended from one edge of the computer monitor to the other, filling the whole screen, and usually with minimal line spacing in between. Not surprisingly, readability on-screen of such texts was often very poor. Fortunately it is now possible for a content creator or designer to exert more control over how type is displayed. Line length can be fixed by the use of tables to constrain column width. Line length can also be determined simply by adding line breaks <BR> to the text where required. Naturally the amount of type contained in a column row depends on the typeface and type size chosen. A general rule of thumb that applies to print as well as on screen is that for maximum readability line length should range from a minimum of about 40 units of set size (or characters) to 65 units of set size. This is very roughly about 8 to 13 words per line. For Times 12 point, this translates approximately to a column row width of 200 pixels to 325 pixels. In Verdana 12 pt, this translates approximately to a column row width of 260 pixels to 410 pixels. So as a general rule of thumb, a column width less than 200 pixels is probably too narrow (unless you are working on a multi-column layout), while one greater than 450 may be too wide.

Leading (so called because in the days of hot metal typesetting, bars of lead were inserted to physically separate lines) or space between lines has not been easy to achieve in web design prior to the implementation of CSS. CSS now gives the possibility to specify line space precisely. The leading for body type should range from approximately 120 per cent to 150 per cent of the type size, depending on the typeface chosen. Again, some degree of eyeballing on different monitors and platforms is needed to achieve satisfactory results.

To achieve some modicum of control over line spacing without resorting to CSS, workarounds need to be found. One way is to insert before a line break an increase in font size by adding the following tag: <FONT SIZE= "+2"></FONT>. Alternatively, an invisible single pixel image can be embedded in-line with vertical space attributes added to generate the requisite space.

Images

A picture, it is often said, is worth a thousand words. On the web, the converse is more often the case, for even simple images can take up the digital space equivalent to hundreds if not thousands of words. A full screen of plain text, for example, say a couple of hundred words, might result in a file size of just 1 K while a small image of no more than 150 pixels by 75 pixels can swell to ten times that size. Nonetheless, the capacity to deliver graphics on the World Wide Web, thus combining text and images in exciting new ways, is certainly one reason why the medium has branched out from its originally narrow user base to reach massive global audiences. Quite simply, in a world that has grown used to colour television, glossy magazines, and books with designed colour photography as a matter of course, the addition of colour images, animated images, even moving images has allowed the web to compete forcefully with other media for our attention.

Creative content on the web most certainly relies on images in great measure to achieve interesting effects. Due to the limitations of typography in HTML, images for typographical elements are widely used on the web. Indeed, whenever a creative typographical element is required, it is likely to be created as a non-editable image file: headlines, vertical and horizontal text banners, textual navigation bars, text buttons and menu choices, animated text, text with drop shadows, initial or drop caps, and pulled quotes.

The use of imagemaps is another powerful feature supported by the web. An imagemap is a graphic image that has designated 'hot points' which when clicked serve as hyperlinks to different sections of that or any other web site. Images furthermore can be made transparent to sit on white or coloured backgrounds as cut-outs. And of course images can be used for tiling backgrounds to add colour, texture or representational or abstract images to a web page or entire web site.

There is not space in this chapter to go into the finer points of preparing graphic images for the web, a topic which many others have already explored in great depth. However, a few basic principles are necessary to keep in mind.

The two most widely used image file formats for the web at present are GIF (Graphics Interchange Format) and JPEG (Joint Photographic Experts Group). Each treats image compression and file size reduction in different ways; as a general rule, the GIF file format is better for graphic images, that is text images, logos, buttons and the like, and JPEG for photographic images, or images where subtlety of tone matters (an exception is small photographic images, which sometimes work better as GIFs than as JPEGs).

The GIF file format is for indexed images up to 8 bits, that is to say images with a maximum of 256 colours. In an 8 bit system, each individual pixel can have a colour value from 0 to 255. Indexing colours to 8-bit, that is to 256, or even less, to the standard web palette of 216 (to ensure cross-platform compatability and minimal 'dithering' of colours), results in considerable reduction of file size. An image can be reduced even further by means of specifying an adaptive palette to say, 5 bits (32 colours) or even 4 bits (16 colours) or less, each successive stage reducing the number of colours as well as file size, though inevitably a point is reached where the visual quality of the image becomes unacceptable.

Bit depth	Colours
1	2
2	4
3	8
4	16
5	32
6	64
7	128
8	256

The JPEG file format works with 24 bit images, and offers varying levels of compression that reduce file size at the expense of image quality not by reducing the number of colours, but by losing image information that relates to subtle colour and tonal differences. The greater the compression, the more information is lost, but the gains are progressively smaller file sizes. On the web, where image quality is limited to a screen resolution of 72 dots per inch, considerable information can be lost in this fashion while still achieving results that are acceptable. Indeed, for those viewing on 8 bit monitors (still the majority of web users), the loss can often be unnoticeable, while the file size reduction is considerable.

The main point to remember is that, whether using GIF or JPEG file formats, images should always be reduced to as small a file size as is visually acceptable. This can only be tested by viewing the image on different monitors, browsers, and platforms.

What images seem to work best on the web? That is hard to say, and some splendid visual effects can be found on any number of web sites. The use of the transparency feature means that a background colour can be chosen in an image to become transparent, thus facilitating the use of cut-out images. Black and white images can work surprisingly well on the web, perhaps because they sometimes come as a welcome contrast to the gaudy colours and images more usually encountered. There is an emerging opus of fine and creative graphics work for items such as navigation buttons and other user interface navigation elements. Yet at the same time, too much slick computer generated artwork can lead to sites appearing sterile and unwelcoming, the product of computer-generated not human design. So the use of photographic images creatively for backgrounds, cut-outs for navigation elements and icons, and for straight illustrations can often make a site seem more welcoming and user-friendly.

Animated images are also supported on the web. This is achieved simply with the assistance of an animation package that enables successive GIF images (or frames in an animated sequence) to be combined into a single image, with a time delay specified between images. The total file size of the combined animated image is the sum of the individual images, though, so care needs to be taken not to introduce unacceptably large files. One of the newer dynamic features of HTML supported by the latest browser versions is Layers, which allows similar animated effects to be achieved.

Colours and colour palettes

On the web, just as typographical decisions often perforce must come down to the lowest common denominator in order to be safe and sure of what your user will see, so is a choice of colours and colour palettes limited to the 216 web-safe colours that are available on most web browsers. It is important to be aware that should you deviate from colours not on this palette, then a user's browser may compensate by 'dithering' or approximating to the nearest colour, often with less than satisfactory results that are difficult to anticipate. Many graphic packages, especially those geared towards web work, will have this web colour palette installed. Alternatively, precise background colours can be specified within the HTML code using the hexadecimal values where white is FFFFFF, black is 000000, yellow FFFF00, red FF0000, navy blue 0000FF, and so on, with each intermediate colour having its own value.

Iconography

Since the web relies on buttons, menus, imagemaps and other such elements for navigating hypertext, a new, non-verbal, visual vocabulary of pictographs is emerging whereby visual icons are used to represent spatial and navigational elements of a web site. These can be as simple as a stylised image of a house for a Home page link, an envelope for e-mail, a shopping trolley for purchasing an item, and so on. Or more elaborate visual metaphors can be created with artefacts and icons representing various elements within that site.

As the web evolves away from its English-language-centric origins to become a truly international, polyglottal medium, then the vocabulary of non-verbal icons that is comprehensible across linguistic barriers is likely to become ever more developed. Pictographical conventions rather like universally comprehensible road signs are evolving now and will continue to do so. At the moment, however, such a universal vocabulary is still a long way from being established, and one problem that remains is finding ways to make icons that may be unique and specific to a site or topic but which can be immediately understood at a glance. The use of visual icons should ultimately depend on common protocols that make them comprehensible intuitively, with no need for translation. If, conversely, a user has to cross-reference back to a Home or Index page to remember what an icon represents, then it has not achieved its primary purpose. This is certainly an area that will evolve and in which considerably more research needs to be done.

Value added, special effects and third-party plug-ins

For the content creator and web designer, considerable creative effects can be achieved by utilising third-party plug-ins supported by the latest browser versions. Among the most widely used include the Shockwave plug-in, which allows the delivery and playing of Macromedia's Director movies, Flash animations, and Freehand Illustrator files; RealPlayer which facilitates the use of streaming audio and video (sound and video that plays as it downloads); and Apple's QuickTime Virtual Reality plug-in, which allows for the use of QuickTime virtual reality, video, and video conferencing. Adobe's PDFViewer plug-in is another third-party alternative that allows Adobe Acrobat Reader to launch from within the web browser window for the cross-platform accessing of PDF files. Many sites now make use of some or all of these plug-ins and quite powerful effects can be achieved.

However, it must be borne in mind that none of these plug-in technologies, at the time of writing, has yet become universally accepted or, perhaps more important, pre-installed on web browser software. Users therefore may still have to install and configure them for themselves, a considerable barrier to their universal uptake though some programmes will detect whether or not plug-ins are available and download and install them if not. Nonetheless, for the content creator, this means that if you choose to use any of them, then you are immediately restricting your potential audience and may even risk both losing and even alienating visitors to your site (or at the least to that section of your site that makes use of such features). Therefore, it is important to be clear about the reasons for using such features: are they integral to the objectives you are trying to achieve with your site? Many sites, one feels, have chosen to use such features simply to be seen to be at the 'cutting edge' of web design, with little or no thought to their audience's requirements or skills level.

Again, it is imperative to consider your intended target audience. Is it web-savvy and interested in making use of interesting technologies? Or would the necessity of having to download and configure a third-party plug-in put off users and encourage them to click elsewhere? At the least, it is essential to be up-front about what your are offering, let users know what they need, and include download links for users to fetch the requisite plug-ins. Point out, too, how long it is likely to take for such plug-in applications to be downloaded (the wait can be considerable for some of the larger applications). Then at least your users know where they stand and they can make an informed decision on whether to proceed or not.

A further point to consider, incidentally, is that when users follow your link to fetch third-party plug-ins, they may leave your web site and not return, thus defeating the purpose of whatever special effect you are trying to achieve. A way to keep your visitor is to have the third-party's web site plug-in page open in a new browser window, thus keeping your window on screen as well.

The use of both javascript and java applets promises the content creator the opportunity to offer special effects and even software applications across platforms and without the need for special third party plug-ins. Simple effects such as swapping images on mouse rollovers, scrolling text, playing sound files, and animations using layers can be achieved, while more complicated applications can be linked to dynamic updating of databases, archiving content, and much more. Both java applets and javascript are supported by the latest browser versions such as Netscape 4.x and Microsoft Internet Explorer 4.x. The downside though is that both may add considerably to file size and subsequent download speeds, so again, such effects and applications should only be used where necessary rather than just for the sake of it. Furthermore, it should be borne in mind that a new generation of web browsers for appliances such as web TV and for hand-held appliances like web phones may not fully support existing versions of java and javascript.

PDF, the alternative to HTML

In Chapter Seven, I urged writers who want to deliver thoughtful, lengthy or creative texts over the web to consider using the PDF file format, giving readers the option to download such texts for printing and reading off-line. PDF should also be considered by content creators when design matters, when it really is essential to deliver content in a form that you know your users will be able to receive as you want them to. Just as PDF allows the delivery of formatted texts, so is it equally useful for the delivery of design-rich documents, illustrations, maps, illustrated catalogues, charts and databases, forms and much more.

Existing content created in word processing, desktop publishing, graphics, database and spreadsheet software packages can easily be repurposed into PDF file format, while content can also be originated especially for PDF file format to be delivered over the web or across other electronic media (CD-Rom, for example). For users to access PDF files, they do, however, need to have Adobe's Acrobat Reader (available free for downloading from the Adobe Systems Inc. web site[5] and also distributed widely with software packages for the delivery of software documentation). Acrobat Reader is cross-platform and versions are available that are suitable for the Mac OS, DOS, UNIX, Windows, Silicon Graphics and other operating systems.

Many of the design issues and difficulties raised in this chapter that concern presentation of content within the limitations of HTML can be solved through the use of PDF. Because a PDF document contains all the information necessary to display it at the user's end, even including fonts, which can be embedded into a document fully or as subsets to be created at the user's end using Adobe Type Manager technology and Adobe's multiple master fonts, then documents with complex layouts, typographical elements, and graphics, can be delivered in near facsimile form, without the content creator having to learn or create any HTML coding whatsoever.

The PDF file format is particularly suitable for the delivery of certain types of documents. As previously noted, one of the most relevant uses is for the delivery of lengthy text documents or documentation that require thoughtful consideration and reading (whether or not design-rich). In such instances, it may be preferable to offer documents in PDF rather than HTML to be downloaded and printed for reading off-line (or indeed to offer both HTML and PDF versions of the same text). The use of the PDF file format, moreover, is a particularly effective medium for those within a closed environment (an academic community, a company intranet, for example) to share documents and information with one another as Acrobat Reader can be distributed to ensure that all are able to access the content.

Design-rich documents that need to keep complicated layouts intact may also be better delivered in PDF than in HTML. Maps, sales catalogues, illustrated books, complex forms (such as multi-column tax returns, application forms, and much else), interactive tutorials, and tabular information such as financial spreadsheets are all being delivered in PDF over the World Wide Web.[6] One frequent use of the format is for the creation and delivery of e-newsletters that make use of multi-column layouts and varied typography. Not only can such electronic publications be delivered in near facsimile form, a further advantage is that such high quality publications can be offered for sale and delivery on a subscription only basis.

The main disadvantage of using PDF is that it is not yet a universally accepted industry standard, so if material is only available in this format then some users will not be able to acces it (if they don't want to download, install and configure Adobe's Acrobat Reader). To use PDF therefore restricts one's potential audience, perhaps considerably. Other disadvantages are that PDF content is not as easy to update as HTML content, which can be easily updated on-the-fly. Nor is PDF content as interactive as HTML; for example, though it is possible to make good looking forms in PDF, for users to complete and submit them on-line requires the further downloading and configuration of Adobe's Forms 3.5 plug-in.

Nonetheless, it is important for content creators to be aware of this useful alternative to HTML. Adobe claims that more than 20 million users now have Acrobat Reader, and it is likely that as the PDF file format becomes ever more widely used, then it will gradually become accepted as a viable alternative file format for the delivery of certain types of content on the World Wide Web.

1 For further information about XML, see W3's XML resource pages: http://www.w3.org/XML/. A useful FAQ factsheet on XML is 'Frequently Asked Questions about the Extensible Markup Language', maintained on behalf of W3's XML Special Interest Group by Peter Flyn (University College Cork): http://www.ucc.ie/xml/

2 SGML is an international standard for defining the structure and content of different electronic document types that is considerably more powerful than HTML, itself a simplified version of SGML created uniquely to describe a single document type specific to the World Wide Web.

3 Microsoft's Fontpack is available at: http://www.microsoft.com/typography/fontpack/default.htm

4 Later versions of Microsoft's Internet Explorer include a range of screen fonts that are installed on a user's system, making such faces as Arial, Verdana, Comic Sans MS, Georgia and others available. But again, using these typefaces may put one in the position of designing for a specific browser at the expense of universality, something certainly to be aware of.

5 Adobe Systems Inc. http://www.adobe.com

6 According to Adobe Systems Inc., over 250,000 web sites now make use of the PDF file format for the delivery of content over the web. Its 'PDF at Work' web site is a self-registered directory of web sites that utilise PDF: http://www.adobe.com/prodindex/acrobat/pdfweb.html

CHAPTER TEN

Content Creation, Responsibilities and the Reader

New media publishing on the web, in all its glorious potential, can indeed be liberating for the content creator as it has never been easier or cheaper to publish and reach a potential world audience. Yet, the prospect of unintermediated publishing raises many questions about content creation, responsibility, freedom of expression, censorship and privacy. As we move into a new age that turns old publishing models upside down, the onus for responsible and indeed ethical publishing values lies with the content creator.

Freedom of expression versus censorship

The cyberworld divides essentially between those who consider that there should be no control whatsoever over content on the web and those who consider that there may well be a need to implement some means to block or control the publication of content that could be deemed to be offensive, obscene or even downright dangerous.

The United Nations 1948 *Universal Declaration of Human Rights* (Article 19) states: 'Everyone has the right to freedom of opinion and expression; this right includes freedom to hold opinions without interference and to seek, receive and impart information and ideas through any medium and regardless of frontiers.' In a world where basic civil liberties, human rights, freedom of expression and democracy can by no means be taken for granted, the Internet, and indeed the World Wide Web, has been a powerful means of giving voice and expression to those with legitimate private and public grievances and campaigns.

Thus the issue of freedom of speech versus censorship of the web is indeed one that has caused considerable debate on a global scale. The ease and relative inexpense of publishing on the web has empowered virtually anyone to become a web publisher, and on the whole we applaud this considerable achievement. A grassroots revolution in the creation and dissemination of published content has taken place as individuals, organisations, niche and special interest groups have found, alongside traditional publishers, media groups, and large and small corporations, the ways and means to make their voices heard. The decentralised, infrastructure-independent nature of the Internet, moreover, has meant that it has proved to be very robust and resilient in repelling any attempts to control or gag the dissemination of such content.

The dilemma, though, is that while applauding a medium that enables the weak or oppressed to find a voice, most free thinking individuals at the same time deplore its use by less than desirable elements of society such as right wing militia, subversive paramilitary groups, racist and terrorist gatherings, neo-Nazi groups, or anti-democratic, politically motivated organisations that act on behalf of authoritarian regimes. The Klu Klux Klan, the World Church of the Creator, the National Alliance all have web sites that promote their own worrying agendas.

Furthermore, while celebrating a medium that grants special interest groups a means of reaching out and bringing together other like-minded parties located anywhere else in the world, we similarly must deplore the spread of child pornography over the web by international rings of paedophiles who abuse its undoubted powers to outwit national and international law enforcers. And if in public we believe strongly and passionately in freedom of speech, in private we cannot help but be terrified at the prospect of our own children stumbling unwittingly on to content that could seriously harm or disturb them.

This area is likely to remain something of an international legal minefield. There have been cases where web domain host companies and individual directors of those companies have been sued for content held on their servers. Yet to censor that same content would bring equal measures of approbation. In a world that has truly become a global village, how is it possible to control the dissemination of content when that which is deemed offensive (or even illegal) in one country could so easily be transferred to a server in another country where no such laws exist? Indeed, the myth of a cosy global village is spectacularly debunked with the realisation that different countries and cultures may have radically different and diametrically opposed attitudes to both freedom of speech as well as to what may or may not be deemed acceptable or illegal content; indeed radically different values and attitudes to published content itself.

The politics of filtering

Yet, the medium, it should be clear by now, is not the message, nor has it ever been. Those who decry the web itself as a pernicious and evil purveyor of offensive, obscene or perversive content (and there are many doom-and-gloomers who do so most vociferously) are little better than the Luddites who blamed and attacked the machines themselves that displaced them of their jobs. In both instances, the media are being confused with the effects that they confer. Indeed, though offensive texts have been published for centuries, few have argued that the book itself should be banned; though blue movies and hardcore pornographic films have existed since virtually the invention of cinema, no one seeks to ban the making and showing of all films.

Nor are many advocating the wholesale banning of the World Wide Web. However, there are many who fear the web and the content on it which they (or their children) might be unwittingly exposed to. And such fears may be very real indeed, for the web is different in the fact that it is almost impossible to control both what is published, as well as who accesses that content. Historically, offensive books have been banned, in extreme and well-publicized cases; pornographic magazines, at the least, consigned to the top shelves of newsagents; blue films given X certificates that preclude minors viewing them. How, effectively, is it possible to control and regulate content on the web? And is it even desirable to do so?

One self-regulating way that the web is beginning to make order if not control of content is through the staking out of digital space under brands that the consumer can come to trust and accept; in such reassuring digital spaces, the reasoning goes, consumers will be confident that content will meet their expectations regarding decency and other criteria. In some cases, service providers have become content providers; companies such as AOL, CompuServe, Microsoft and others offer their own specially commissioned content available only to subscribers. In other cases, content providers are creating portal sites that help to brand their collections of web sites under an umbrella grouping that web users will come to trust, not only for the provision of decent content, but equally important for the provision of authoritative content that they can rely on. Such branding, sometimes based on existing media brands (TimeWarner, Walt Disney Online), but more usually on original new media and corporate 'imprints' is a feature that will continue to emerge. But does this mean that as a result, small individual sites may find it increasingly harder to compete? And is leaving the matter to corporate market forces really the answer?

Mechanisms already do exist, and are evolving, for the effective filtering of content. PICS (Platform for Internet Content Selection) is a protocol created by the W3 consortium in order to find ways to label content so that that which is offensive, while not being banned, can be filtered out by those organisations or individuals who want to do so. Today there are a number of commercial products making use of this protocol that will filter out content based on a variety of criteria: partial nudity, full nudity, gross depictions, sexual acts, alcohol, drugs, offensive language, and so on. The HateFilter, launched in November 1998 by the Anti-Defamation League (ADL), is a tool that blocks access to a continually updated list of web sites run by racist groups.

The problem, as with any type of censorship, is, and has always has been, who do we trust to make the decisions and subjective value judgements as to what is, or is not, acceptable? What is deemed pornographic by one person may well be another's recreational activity. Those who are most vociferous in their championing of censorship of the web, moreover, have traditionally come from right wing sectors of society that have been less than liberal in their values and judgements of lifestyle. Thus, gay and lesbian sites might well be blocked or filtered out as well as public welfare sites offering information and support for HIV positive sufferers. Meanwhile those cybernannies who think that reading about alcohol is likely to turn us all into hopeless alcoholics might well find a way to turn off responsible sites that deal with subjects like wine. Such cyberfilters, it should be added, are far from sophisticated and in many cases may be unable to intelligently distinguish the acceptable from the unacceptable. Indeed, there have been instances of hamfisted filters blocking sites with the word 'breast', thus not only depriving users of the human female form, but effectively banning food sites with recipes that include the chicken variety. Clearly filtering of this type, if imposed from the top down, that is by governments or even by service providers themselves, may be not only unacceptable but also ineffective.

On the other hand, filters that can be chosen to be used out of personal preference may be of more interest and use to individuals. Responsible organisations producing such products would gain the trust of consumers who share their values and a large range of criteria could be built into such systems. Businesses, for example, might choose to filter out all recreational and consumer sites (not just pornographic ones) in order to maintain greater employee productivity. Those individuals, meanwhile, with more liberal or radical views about what is or is not offensive could choose themselves to use filters that reflect their own views, or indeed choose not to use any filters at all. As XML (Extensible Markup Language) becomes fully implemented, finer and more intelligent meta-information that will distinguish types of content will be able to be built into web documents in order to assist in this process, something that will be welcomed.

The real problem with filtering content is when one segment of society wishes to impose its own values and views on another. Recent cases involving public libraries in the United States have highlighted this inherent dilemma. Many public libraries offer access to the World Wide Web. What happens when their publicly funded and accessible computer terminals have the potential to be used to access offensive or pornographic content? What happens when those who are able to access such content may be minors, indeed our own children?

Not surprisingly there have been calls for the filtering or even banning of public Internet use by those who fear the medium and all that it represents. Real potential danger undoubtedly does exist. But the dilemma must be how to balance freedom of speech and the right of access of content for adults with the very real need to protect children and other vulnerable elements of society.

Some libraries, faced with this dilemma, have tried to encourage responsible Internet use, while others have resorted to using filters. A compromise approach is to have some machines available that are unfiltered, but which are placed in a private area where content accessed on them will not be visible to others, and which are out of bounds to children or minors. The danger, though, is that such machines, rather like adult arcade peekaboo shows in Soho, may become the domain of perverts.[1]

An alternative approach is, instead of filtering content, to put the onus on the user to be responsible. For example, Devon County Council has adopted an unequivocal approach: minors under the age of 16 can only access the World Wide Web on library computers if accompanied by a responsible adult (such as a parent or carer) for the duration of the search. And, while not filtering content, it places responsibility on the user not to abuse the system and indeed to stay on the right side of the law, pointing out that under obscene publications legislation and the Telecommunications Act of 1984, users may be liable to prosecution if they intentionally use library computers 'to download, upload, look at, read, distribute, circulate or sell any material which is pornographic, obscene, grossly offensive or violent.'[2]

The onus is being placed on the individual to be responsible, even though we all know that in many instances this may not be realistic. As for the content creator? So must there be a similar responsibility, foremost to inform a potential or target audience as to what they are likely to receive in a web site. A responsibility, too, to ensure that adult and other potentially offensive sites do not target or seek to attract vulnerable groups or minors.

Meanwhile, for those who believe unreservedly in the right of freedom of speech, there must equally be an acceptance that offensive content of all types and degrees will continue to be created and to proliferate on the web, as in other media. For those who advocate filtering, it should be similarly acknowledged that even if imposed from on top or offered as a matter of personal choice, filtering of content may still amount to little more than looking the other way, or burying one's head in the virtual sand.

Freedom of speech versus censorship is a difficult issue and one that needs to be explored, questioned, and grappled with by responsible content creators, by web users, indeed by all free thinkers alike.

Copyright, plagiarism and unfair practices

The World Wide Web, in its facility through the hyperlink to bring together related content, articles and web sites, contains within it the mechanisms for potential and real infringement of intellectual property rights. Indeed, a web site without hyperlinks is a very bare one indeed, and an argument running throughout this book is that content on the web differs from traditional linear content in the richness that such horizontal and vertical relational hyperlinks add. A web site on any given subject can expand and amplify its depth of content not necessarily by researching and creating unique and original content itself but simply by linking to other existing web sites that cover that ground, and without even asking permission from that site's creator to do so. Generally, few content creators, moreover, seem to object, as links to and from a site are an accepted convention of web publishing.

In the early days when the web was non-commercial, something of a communal spirit of generosity reigned between content creators, allied with a seemingly inherent culture of sharing: content, like knowledge, was there to be passed around and nobody seemed to be too overly possessive about it. The web browser, after all, offers the built-in facility to display a content creator's raw HTML code, thus effectively offering for gratis the complex inner structure of a web site that a designer may have taken days or weeks to create.

Now that the web has become big business, unscrupulous practices have begun to creep in. The technology that has empowered individuals and organisations to become publishers with minimal distribution costs has, at the same time, facilitated digitial commercial piracy on a scale never before imaginable or conceivable. Indeed, it has never been so easy both to steal, as well as to distribute globally that stolen material, all at the mere touch of a button or two. Content can be copied and pasted and so does not usually need even to be re-keyed in; colour images and complex graphics can be lifted; and documents can be distributed without recourse to a printing press or even so much as a photocopier. Indeed, as in other media where the stealing of intellectual property through the pirating of books, magazines, audio CDs, and videos is a multimillion dollar international problem yet to be solved, the stealing of content on the Internet has become a real and vexing problem.

Moreover, there may be considerably more subtle grey areas where it is not always clear where the sharing of content crosses over that fine line between acceptable conduct and copyright infringement. If, for example, you come across an interesting site and e-mail a friend or colleague its URL, then that is fine. But should you copy and paste an article or snippet of content from that site and send it by e-mail (and technologically it is possible to do so with the greatest ease to any number of e-mail addresses, say hundreds or even thousands, thus in effect republishing that material), then technically you are infringing copyright, just as you would be if you made multiple photocopies of a newspaper or magazine article to share with others. It would probably be impossible to enforce such an infringement, and indeed, in those cases where people are sharing content but not actually making money out of doing so, then a blind eye is often, though not always, turned (the concept of 'fair use' is based on common sense – small sections of works can be quoted without the copyright holder's permission).

The practice known as 'framing' can be a more dubious if not downright illegal means of lifting content. In web site design, frames are used to allow a screen to display two or more pages of information; the frames can display information from within the same site, or they may contain information from different, external sites hyperlinked by their URLs. Thus, by creating a navigational frame that gives a site its thematic and corporate identity, then causing content from another site to open within that site's main body window, users can be deluded into thinking that the content itself originated from the original site creator, especially since its title, site address and contact information may appear prominently at the 'top' of the page. There have been recent legal cases[3] where just such occurrences have taken place. So-called news filtering services seek to offer content from a variety of sources simply by collecting hyperlinks to them, while framing that content so that it appears within the site's own windows. Clearly, if this same thing happened in print, then it would be a blatant case of plagiarising. However it is not yet conclusive by any means whether or not framing is technically illegal (it will certainly vary from individual instance to instance), though in many cases it may certainly be morally so.

Furthermore, while the sharing of URLs of other sites may be acceptable and indeed an essential part of the web, the use of 'deep' hyperlinks to stories or content buried within web sites may not always be acceptable. In giving deep hyperlinks, content can be accessed without users having to go through the linked site's Home page; if the site was funded by advertising on that Home page, then such a deep link could result in the potential loss of revenue.[4] In other cases, unscrupulous content creators have registered misleading domain names that are similar to the names of rival or popular companies in order to attract users unwittingly to their own site or sites.

The use of the <META> tag, that is, the invisible informative tag that is included in web sites for robot search engines to catalogue, is another area open to abuse. Commercial sites can put in names and descriptions of their competitors so that when someone types in that name or description, then their site comes up alongside, ahead of, or sometimes even instead of the competitor's site. Protected names and trademarks may also be used in such invisible <META> tags to attract users to a site in an unwarranted or misleading way.[5]

It is important for the content creator to be aware of some of these issues to avoid falling foul of both accepted ethics and the law, which is still very much evolving on these matters as cases are brought to the fore. And certainly it may also be reassuring for content creators to know that should their work be plagiarised or infringed upon in any of these or other ways, then there may be legal recourse to protect their electronic intellectual property rights.

Such issues, though, need to be kept in perspective. Most content creators need not fear that there are cyber-thieves waiting anxiously for their next new content to appear in order to pinch it. Yet in conducting workshops with writers, a recurring concern I have come across is the fear that by publishing on the web, one's work will suddenly be at the mercy of all those unscrupulous pirates that lie out there in wait, ready to pounce and plagiarise at will. That incipient novel that you've been working on for the past six years might all of a sudden appear verbatim under the name or pseudonym of someone else. Well, yes, perhaps this could in theory happen. In practice, the sheer surplus of content on the World Wide Web is likely to be a major self-regulating force. For indeed one of the greatest challenges is not in creating more content, but in finding a way to filter and distinguish the most valid from the merely self-indulgent.

It should be reassuring, too, for content creators to know that there may be electronic means to protect content. Digital watermarking can be carried out on images, photographs and graphics, whereby invisible codes are embedded thus identifying the creator, copyright holder and/or any other relevant information. Should a user wish to reproduce that image, then he can get in contact with the creator or copyright holder and negotiate a fee. Perhaps we will even find means to renumerate content creators whose work is 'borrowed'. Just as it may be possible to filter acceptable and unacceptable content using tags to identify, say, adult sites, so may it be possible to use such tags (or meta-information available in XML) to identify commercial content (images or text) when it is accessed and downloaded, so that the content creator automatically receives a micropayment from the e-account of the user.

What is clear is that the technology of the web is challenging us to reconsider the way we view and interact with intellectual property. It is likely that this process will continue to evolve with the web.

Ethics, morality and the web

Can a medium have its own morality? Certainly there may be moralities that become associated with specific media. Witness the types of content, illustrations and language that are acceptable for a tabloid newspaper in Britain as compared to those that are acceptable for a broadsheet (though there are those who would argue that the gap is lessening between the two). The morality of adult cinemas in Soho may differ from that of the Odeons in suburbia. Books and magazines from certain publishers may have a morality that differs from books and magazines by other publishers. Daytime television has a morality that is different from television after the nine p.m. watershed.

The World Wide Web, in fact, may in its present form be unique in its amorality. Mature traditional media have long established their own hierarchies and conventions as to what is acceptable or not acceptable, here or there, now, then or later; we can choose to go to Soho for certain types of entertainment, or pick our magazines from the top shelf of the newsagents, or watch violent or adult content on television later in evening. On the web, by contrast, all content may be deemed equal: the top shelf equivalent web sites nestle cheek-by-jowl with academic, scientific, commercial or entertainment sites, or for that matter sites devoted to freedom fighters or political agitators or racists or terrorists, all equally accessible by their unique URLs.

Yet one senses that a morality of web publishing is emerging and evolving, as the medium itself matures and users – content creators and accessors alike – strive to find a path that ensures the whole thing keeps on functioning, hopefully efficiently yet responsibly, void of any control imposed from on top. It does seem certain that some means will need to evolve in order to identify, and thus place on the electronic top shelf out of view of most decent folks, those sites that are gratuitously obscene and pornographic. It is not a question of banning such sites, as well as others too that are offensive for whatever reasons, but rather of creating a hierarchy so that people know where to find or avoid them, just as we know not to buy certain newspapers or magazines if we don't want to view topless women or bottomless men. The establishment of trusted brands or web imprints that users will come to rely on for decent and authoritative content may be one way to achieve this. Perhaps too eventually an acceptable form of ratings will evolve, rather like the ratings for movies.[6]

The danger always, though, is where will regulation, whether voluntary or imposed, stop? Authoritarian countries are already regulating the types of content that they allow their citizens to publish (and indeed access) on the web. Under the guise of morality and protection (of minors, citizens, or whoever), controls may be imposed that aim to gag a medium that is historically most noteworthy in its democratic granting of a voice to all and sundry, whatever their views, politics, or sexual preferences. It must be hoped that the web itself – and the underlying infrastructure of the Internet on which it relies to function – will be sufficiently resilient enough to resist any such attempts to silence or control it.

There are other issues relating to the ethics and morality of web publishing. Because it is so easy to publish on the web, many have used the medium for their own personal ends, often to attack individuals or organisations. In some cases, the medium provides an outlet and a voice for legitimate grievances and injustices that would otherwise go unheard. In other cases, unjustified personal sniping and mad obsession finds an outlet that can do real damage to both individuals and organisations. The hyperlink that is the basis of the World Wide Web can be used as a powerful and sometimes irresponsible weapon. Negative, diatribal sites may point to the object of their grievances in nasty, damaging, and downright unfair ways. Indeed, the web is used to convey libellous sentiments and often defamation of character that would not be tolerated in print, and it is certainly only a matter of time before we see more and more litigious precedents as to what is and what is not acceptable practice on the web. I can already hear the lawyers rubbing their hands in glee at the prospect.

By using the web as a powerful tool to give voice to grievances and injustices, political platforms can be created for oppressed and dispossessed peoples around the world. In the last year, we've witnessed the effective use of the medium in Mexico, Kosovo, Indonesia, Kashmir, China and elsewhere. The medium itself, though, is apolitical, and can be equally exploited to give voice to government or opposition propaganda. Such efforts, whatever their point of view and irregardless of whether or not we agree with the content itself, use the medium in an essentially constructive fashion, that is, to promote or voice an agenda, political point of view, or argument. Recently, however, a new destructive phenomenon has arisen, so-called 'hacktivism' whereby politically motivated hackers attack the web sites of persons, companies, institutions or governments that they deem to be responsible for their own particular grievances. Host computers are infiltrated, new sometimes embarrassing pages are put up, or existing pages are altered or destroyed; or sites can even be made to crash catastrophically. Proponents call such actions a new form of electronic civil disobedience, but it should be pointed out that such web savvy tactics may be available to those on all sides of the political spectrum. In Serbia recently a group called Black Hand vandalised both Albanian and Croatian web sites; Croatian hackers responded by attacking key Serbian sites. Ethnic wars, it seems, may be now waged digitally as well as physically and morally.

Even within a democracy, the ethics of what is acceptable or unacceptable may be far from clear. When the Republican-dominated House of Representatives decided to publish Kenneth Starr's long awaited report on President Clinton's affairs, in all its meticulously salacious detail, one could not help but question the motives for doing so, the seeming abdication of moral authority jettisoned under the politically motivated guise of 'freedom of speech'. The feeding-frenzy mentality that resulted overspilled into other media too. Indeed, without the impetus of the Starr Report on the web, I doubt whether there would have been such an eagerness on the part of the House to release the videotapes of Clinton's testimony to the grand jury.

The whole sordid business raises another issue about the ethics of web publishing. The Clinton/Lewinsky story was first reported on Matt Drudge's 'Drudge Report'.[7] Drudge is a champion of 'unedited' information and content, often reporting on reports rather than on the events themselves. This means that while at times he has sometimes been able to respond more quickly than traditional media in breaking 'newsworthy' stories, at the same time, his reports have often been proved to be wildly wrong, sometimes damagingly so (though not in this case).

Drudge's approach to web journalism raises questions about the ethics of publishing unedited or unintermediated content on the web. Editors, after all, have traditionally existed to serve as human filters of content, to ensure that stories are of public interest, have been checked, and are accurate before being filed and published, that they do not unfairly attack an individual's character, and that, hopefully, professional journalistic ethics are maintained. But there is no room for such traditional editorial safeguards in the unintermediated approach to web journalism. Drudge would furthermore claim that the number of visitors to his site proves that this is an approach that the public appreciates. Thus, the morality of publishing unedited content on the web represents a fundamental shift in the ethics, power and responsibility of the journalist.

Does this mean that there can be no ethics relating to web publishing? In a world of unedited and unintermediated content, where gossip and innuendo can be given as fact, is there no longer any onus on the content creator to be truthful and honest and fair and careful? Of course there is. The ethics of publishing in a free society must remain rooted above all in our collective sense of fairness, decency and basic human values, irregardless of whether Matt Drudge or the tabloid newspapers would have us believe otherwise. That is not to say that journalists, authors and web authors don't sometimes overstep the bounds of such unwritten ethics, often consciously and even contemptuously so; such has long been the case with tabloid journalism long before the advent of the web, though historically there has still been the safeguard of overall editorial judgement and the very real threat of litigation. On the web, though, it may well be far easier and quicker for the unscrupulous, the scurrilous, the unprofessional content creator to publish unethical, untruthful, or scandalous content and get away with it. It is likely, indeed even imperative, that in the future we will have to see legislation, both on a national and an international scale, to compel content creators to be responsible and maintain professional ethics relating to defamation of character, libel, and privacy, or else risk litigation.

Web users may not even be willing to wait for such legislation, but prefer instead to undertake direct action themselves. A tactic that has long been in place, often utilised as a response to commercial enterprises that have attempted to infiltrate non-commercial user discussion groups, is 'flaming'. It is probable that other means of direct action by web users themselves are likely to evolve as a means of retaliating against those who are deemed to be unfair, indecent, or, more likely who have abused the unwritten commercial rules of the system.[8]

Privacy versus the public

If each new medium is but an extension of ourselves, it is worth considering the implications of web publishing in relation to our private and public selves and indeed to basic civil liberties in the electronic information age.[9]

Publishing on the web truly allows us as individuals to project ourselves publicly and on a global scale never before achievable. It grants individuals, organisations, companies, political groupings, we've said, a voice that can be heard, sometimes loud and clear like a clarion rallying cry around the world.

But such a projection of ourselves, our ideas, and our ideals can sometimes backfire too. In rushing out to publish our personal, private or public manifestos we may consciously or unwittingly provide the mechanism and opportunity for others to infiltrate our private lives in a way that we may have neither considered nor wished. Publishing, by its very nature and no matter what the medium, is a public act: that of taking private thoughts and opinions and laying them out for others to read, comment on, or act upon. It is a public act that often leads in unexpected directions, never more so than on the web. You never know who may be out there perusing your web pages, perhaps sympathetically, but perhaps not. It is not so much that Big Brother may be watching; he is probably not, for Orwell's nightmare scenario has yet to come to pass (though many fear that the hardwire infrastructure that will bring interactive web TV into our living rooms may provide a mechanism for it to do so). Rather, more worrying, a hundred baby brothers, or just one lone weirdo or pervert may be out there waiting to pounce. Or, even more likely, a hundred or more junk e-mailers may be tracking your web surfing patterns in order to target you with a barrage of unsolicited e-mail compiled by a so-called 'intelligent' spider robot that thinks it can anticipate your needs and desires even before you yourself do.

For indeed, when users visit a web page, we leave behind a number of private facts of potential interest and value to others: the country and sometimes city that we access from; the type of computer used; browser software; the precise time of day that the site was accessed; our IP addresses which can be used to find out our e-mail addresses; the route that brought us to that page; and much more. A web site host can insert a 'cookie' into our browsers to record information relevant to our browsing habits that can then be transmitted back to the host. Javascripts can be written to extract information such as e-mail addresses and postal addresses. Such information may be utilised legitimately in order to assist web site creators to gain a portrait of their actual audience, and to assist in shaping content to fit that audience. But the same information has the undoubted potential to be used irresponsibly or in ways that we as individuals might well not desire, whether for commercial or marketing initiatives or possibly even by governments to learn about and track our interests, patterns, even whereabouts. Indeed, without getting unduly paranoic, it is not impossible to imagine how such information could be used for unscrupulous or downright sinister purposes. It is in such potential instances of abuse that fundamental issues such as the right to privacy come to the fore.[10]

It is just as well to remain aware of the potential sinister power of the medium, and to protect and keep private that which you don't want to become part of the public domain. Children, for example, should never divulge their real names, phone numbers or addresses to others over the web; nor, for that matter, should most adults unless they have good reason for doing so. There have already been cases of abusive and perverted cyber-stalkers who have harassed and followed their victims through cyberspace and sometimes into the real physical world. It should always be remembered that content posted on the web so easily from the intimate comfort of our bedrooms or offices may be laid bare for all and sundry to see and consider; even private e-mails and postings on newsgroups may find their way somehow into the public domain. In a world that is ever more prurient, less mindful of privacy and the rights of the individual, the need to be vigilant is ever greater.

There are moves for government involvement to assist in maintaining the rights of privacy of individuals. A new European Union directive put into effect on 26 October 1998 aims to prohibit the buying and selling of personal data. Companies furthermore would be compelled to give individuals access to information held about themselves. And they would be prohibited from transmitting any such personal data to any country that does not have similar privacy protection guarantees in legislative place, most notably the United States where such controls have been resisted to date, though there are indications that the Clinton adminstration may have to look at the issue of privacy of digital information again in the light of the European ruling.

Even without government assistance, there are tools that can assist the individual in maintaining privacy. Programmes can help a user to surf anonymously, ensuring that no private information is divulged without permission and blocking out the laying of 'cookies' or the running of javascripts and java applets.[11] For those concerned about the privacy of e-mail, the services of a re-mailer can be enlisted whereby e-mails are sent and received by a third party who then encrypts and resends them anonymously. And there are tools that add security to FTP and telnet transactions and furthermore can encrypt your browser as well as your entire hard disk, should you worry about hackers infiltrating your computer. Such means of protecting privacy and the consumer are likely to be developed further quickly, not least driven by the corporate demands of e-commerce and the need for transactions over the web to be not only secure, but to be seen to be secure in order to attract mass consumers.

Yet while it may be reassuring for the web user to know that there may be ways and means to protect privacy, the onus must equally lie with content creators not to abuse their audiences. Individuals who come to a web site may inevitably and unwittingly leave their electronic footprints behind. Someone who has visited an adult site in the privacy of his or her home, however, should be able to expect that e-mail addresses will not be divulged to all and sundry any more than the consumer who has visited a commercial site wants his e-mail address to be shared with others. The privacy of the visitor, no matter what the subject of the site, needs to be respected and considered, and there needs to be a strong ethical code, preferably backed up by legislation, relating to the sharing of e-mail addresses and electronic databases.

Final thoughts

The World Wide Web is still in its infancy as a publishing and communications medium, and it is likely that it will continue to evolve at its present meteoric rate. In great measure, this process of evolution is driven by new technologies. As radically different appliances are developed and put into production, as new means and ways of accessing the web come into widespread use, as HTML further evolves and XML comes into full implementation, the types of content published on the World Wide Web will naturally change considerably to adapt to a changing medium. For example, content developed for a 17 inch or even a 14 inch computer screen will need to be altered to be accessible on a monitor linked to some form of electronic hand-held book, the microwave/web browser in the kitchen, web TV, or a hand-held combination mobile phone and web browser. New technologies, furthermore, will assist us in filtering out undesirable content, should we so desire, and in keeping our private lives private as much as possible and desirable.

Meanwhile worthwhile local content, and increasingly non-English language content, will be developed for individual countries, regions, localities, while niche content on specialist subjects will proliferate at the same time as multinational brands attempt to establish an electronic cyberpresence as all-pervasive as the multinational brands that exist in the physical world. Issues such as electronic civil liberties, freedom of speech, and the use of the medium to promote democracy and human rights are threatened to be overshadowed by the commercial and corporate concerns of multinational companies whose only interest is the bottom line profit at the end of it all.

The prospects are at once exciting and terrifying. Where will it all end? Or rather, on what journey have we embarked, and where will it all take us? It is hard to say but what is certain is that there is no point in burying one's head in the sand and hoping or denying that this medium is not going to change us. Just as the telephone, radio and television altered our perceptions and identities, our very concept of ourselves as human beings, so will the World Wide Web spread its net ever more comprehensively and pervasively into and within our public and private lives.

Already it's hardly possible to keep up with the speed of changes that the web is bringing. Yet there also comes a time when we need to step back from it all, forget about the technology that drives the Internet, the gizmos and plug-ins, browser wars and e-commerce, privacy and pornography. Indeed there comes a time when we simply need to turn away from our computer monitors to return to our basic values rooted in centuries of thought and knowledge.

For ultimately the World Wide Web, as a publishing and communications medium, is no more, no less than an outlet that allows us to express our concerns, hopes, fears, aspirations and enthusiasms; to reflect at this moment in time and space on what it is to be alive on this planet at the end of the second millennium; to voice our thoughts; and to be heard. The basic values common to the human condition, as well as the baser values, are all, and will all be reflected and projected in this medium as they have been in all the other media that have preceded it from time immemorial.

Fundamental questions of ethics, values and the morality of publishing on the World Wide Web will continue to arise, but so long as we can turn our attentions to them from within the context of this sound and long-established humanistic framework that is the cornerstone of our civilisation then I remain reasonably confident that we will be able to find answers to most of them.

1 In an interesting and significant ruling on 23 November 1998, a federal judge struck down the policy of the Loudoun County, Virginia library system to filter content from its library computer terminals. At the core of the judgement was the view by Judge Leonie M. Brinkema, that such a policy offends the guarantee of free speech. As reported in the *NY Times Cybertimes*, 23 November 1998. http://www.nytimes.com/library/tech/98/11/cyber/articles/ Similarly on 14 January 1999, a judge in Northern California dismissed a lawsuit seeking to suspend Internet access at a local public library if it continued to provide public access to material deemed harmful to minors. As reported in the *NY Times Cybertimes*, 14 January 1999. http://www.nytimes.com/library/tech/99/01/cyber/articles/15library-day.html
2 Leaflet 7296, 'Using Library Computers', July 1998, Devon County Council,UK.
3 *Washington Post v. Total News* and *The Journal Gazette v. Fort Wayne Newspapers Inc.* have been two recent cases in the United States that have involved the issue of 'framing' content.
4 An article that examines some of these issues is: Jeffrey R. Kuester, Peter A. Nieves, 1998. 'Hyperlinks, Frames and Meta-tags: An Intellectual Property Analysis', *IDEA: The Journal of Law and Technology*. http://www.patentperfect.com/idea.htm. The case of deep hyperlinking refers to *Shetland Times Ltd. v. Dr. Jonathan Wills and Zetnews Ltd.*
5 Adult sites, for example, often include words such as Playboy or Penthouse in their <META> tags, thus infringing on the rights of those magazines.
6 The UK's Internet Watch Foundation (IWF), the body charged with pursuing web users' complaints about web content, is attempting to come up with an international ratings system that will be able to rate web pages that would be acceptable in different countries, reflecting on concerns that exist within different cultures. The proposed Internet Content Rating Alliance (ICRA) will be composed of representives from the IWF as well as from other national equivalent bodies. Further information from: http://www.isf.org.uk
7 The Drudge Report is at: http://www.drudgereport.com
8 The American anti-impeachment web site Move On is an example of a grassroots movement in which some thousands of individuals are giving voice to their collective feelings and also taking direct action by donating considerable funds to help candidates in future elections to unseat those who have voted for impeachment. http://www.MoveOn.org

9 An organisation that deals with the issue of privacy and the Internet is EPIC (Electronic Privacy Information Network). On its web site there are a number of resources and articles relating to legislation, means of protecting privacy on the Internet and much else. http://epic.org

10 The Global Internet Liberty Campaign has conducted a survey on 'privacy and human rights' in some 50 countries, and presents some startling results. http://www.gilc.org/

11 Anonymizer, Inc. for example is one such company that claims to provide 'comprehensive identity privacy and anonymity services for ultimate secure, private, anonymous Internet use.' http://www.anonymizer.com/privacy/survey/

A late breaking development as we go to press (26/3/99) is that Nato's bombing of Serbia and Kosovo has resulted in a clampdown on independent news reporting and Internet discussion of the situation, with worrying reports of seizures, arrests and atrocities. In order to protect those who use the Internet, Anonymizer.com has offered its services through the Kosovo Privacy Project: 'In response to requests from the human rights community, Anonymizer has set up two special services to handle the needs of Kosovars, Serbs, and others reporting on the current situation in Kosovo. Any Internet posting carries with it grave privacy concerns. In this case, a breach of privacy could be life threatening. We see two immediate needs: first, anonymous email, and second, anonymous access to information and discussions. We already offer free anonymous e-mail through our Mixmaster Web Interface, but the delay of up to two days may be too long in a crisis like this. To address this we have created a secure anonymous e-mail interface with no delay. Anyone in the world can already use our free Anonymizer Surfing. We have now removed the delay on Kosovo related web sites and news sources to make access easier for those who need this service.' Further information at: http://info.anonymizer.com/kosovo.shtml

Further Reading

Aronson, Larry, *HTML 3 Manual of Style,*(ZD Press, Emeryville, 1995).

Birkerts, Sven, *The Gutenberg Elegies The Fate of Reading in an Electronic Age,*(Faber & Faber, London, 1996).

Bonhime, Andrew, Pohlmann, Ken C., *Writing for New Media,* (John Wiley & Sons, New York, 1998).

Coupland, Ken, ed., *Graphis Web Design Now 1,* (Graphis U.S. Inc., New York, 1997).

den Boer, Liesbeth, Strengholt, Geert J., Velthoven, Willem, eds., *Website Graphics,* (Thames & Hudson, London, 1997).

Dyson, Esther, *Release 2.0 A Design for Living in the Digital Age,* (Broadway Books, New York, 1997).

Earnshaw, R., Vince, J., Jones, H eds., *Digital Media and Electronic Publishing,* (Academic Press, London, 1996).

Gates, Bill, *The Road Ahead,* (Viking, London, 1995).

Howard, Bruce, *The Writers' Web,* (Abacus, Grand Rapids, 1997).

Johnson, Steven, *Interface Culture,* (HarperCollins, San Francisco, 1997).

McAleese, Ray, ed., *Hypertext Theory into Practice,* (Intellect Books, Oxford, 1993).

McLuhan, Marshall, *Understanding Media The Extensions of Man,* (MIT Press, Cambridge, MA, first published 1964 (reissue) 1994).
The Global Village Transormations in World Life and Media in the 21st Century, (Oxford University Press, New York, 1986).

McLuhan, Marshall, Fiore, Quentin, *The Medium is the Massage An Inventory of Effects,* (Hardwired, San Francisco, 1967, renewed 1996).

Negroponte, Nicholas, *Being Digital,* (Hodder & Stoughton, London, 1995).

Nyce, James, M. and Kahn, Paul, eds., *From Memex to Hypertext – Vannevar Bush and the Mind's Machine*, (Academic Press, London, 1991).

O'Donnell, James J., *Avatars of the World*, (Harvard University Press, Cambridge, 1998).

Page, Bruce, Holm, Diana, *Web Publishing with Adobe Acrobat and PDF,* (John Wiley & Sons, New York, 1996).

Partridge, Derek & Rowe, Jon, *Computers and Creativity*, (Intellect Books, Oxford, 1994).

Pfaffenberger, Bryan, *The Elements of Hypertext Style*, (Academic Press, London, 1997).

Postman, Neil, *Technopoly The Surrender of Culture to Technology*, (Vintage Books, New York, 1993).

Rheingold, Howard, *The Virtual Community*, (Secker & Warburg, London, 1994).

Schwartz, Evan I., *Webonomics*, (Penguin, Harmondsworth, 1997).

Siegel, David, *Creating Killer Web Sites*, (Hayden Books, Indianopolis, 1996).

Tapscott, Don, *Growing Up Digital The Rise of the Net Generation,* (McGraw Hill, New York, 1998).

Web References

'As We May Think' (electronic edition of article by Vannevar Bush) – http://www.isg.sfu.ca/~duchier/misc/vbush/

Adobe Acrobat and PDF – http://www.adobe.com/proindex/acrobat//main.html

Adobe Systems – http://www.adobe.com

After Emmett – http://net22.com/qazingulaza/joglars/afteremmett/bonvoyage.html

Afterlife – http://www.afterlife.org

AltaVista – http://www.altavista.com

Amazon.com – http://www.amazon.com

Anonymizer, Inc. – http://www.anonymizer.com

Anti-Rascist.com – http://www.antiracist.com/

Ask Jeeves – http://www.askjeeves.com

BBC On-line – http://www.bbc.co.uk

Beeb@the BBC – http://www.beeb.com

Center of the Java Universe – http://java.sun.com

CGI Collection – http://www.itm.com/cgicollection/

Coffeehouse Writings from the Web – http://www.coffeehousebook.com/

Concise, Scannable, and Objective: How to Write for the Web –
http://www.useit.com/papers/webwriting/writing.html

Creating Killer Web Sites – http://www.killersites.com

CSS Gallery – http://www.microsoft.com/truetype/css/gallery/entrance.htm

Data Protection Registrar – http://www.dpr.gov.uk/

The Drudge Report – http://www.drudgereport.com

The Elements of Style by William Strunk, Jr. –
http://www.columbia.edu/acis/bartleby/strunk/

EPIC (Electronic Privacy Information Network) – http://epic.org

Extensible Markup Language (XML) – http://www.w3.org/XML/

Frequently Asked Questions about the Extensible Markup Language – http://www.ucc.ie/xml

Gamelan – Java Resources – http://www.gamelan.com

Global Internet Liberty Campaign – http://www.gilc.org/

The Globe – http://www.theglobe.com

GVU's WWW User Surveys – http://gvu.gatech.edu/user_surveys/

Homer Homepage – http://www.dc.peachnet.edu/~shale/humanities/literature/world_literature/homer.html

HTML Writers Guild – http://www.hwg.org/

ICQ Internet Online Communication Network – http://www.icq.com/icqhomepage.html

InfoSeek – http://www.infoseek.com

Internet Watch Foundation (IWF) – http://www.isf.org.uk

Jakob Nielson's Alert Box – http://www.useit.com/alertbox/

Java Applet Library – http://www.applets.com

Java Home Page – http://www.javasoft.com

Jennicam – http://www.jennicam.org

The Kenyon Review – http://www.kenyonreview.com

Lycos Search – http://www.lycos.com

Lynx – http://www.lynx.browser.org

Macromedia – http://www.macromedia.com

Mosaic – http://www.ncsa.uiuc.edu/SDG/Software/Mosaic/

Metajournals – http://www.metajournals.com

Mosaic – http://www.ncsa.uiuc.edu/SDG/Software/Mosaic/

Nerve Magazine – http://www.Nerve.com/

Neverending Tale – http://www.coder.com/creations/tale/

New York Times – http://www.nytimes.com/

Often: Almost Daily Journal Entries – http://www.ounce.com/often/

Opera – http://www.operasoftware.com

The Palace – http://www.thepalace.com

Project Gutenberg – http://promo.net/pg/

RealAudio – http://www.realaudio.com

Rheingold's Brainstorms – http://www.rheingold.com/

Tango – http://www.alis.com

Shockwave – http://www.macromedia.com/shockwave/

Suck – http://www.suck.com

Sun Guide to Web Style – http://wwwwseast2.usec.sun.com/styleguide/

The Virtual Community – http://www.rheingold.com/vc/book/

World Wide Web Consortium (W3) – http://www.w3.org

Urban Desires – http://www.desires.com/

Visual Poetry – http://www1.shore.net/~gmahoney/

Visual Thesaurus – http://www.plumbdesign.com/thesaurus/

W3 HTML Validation Service – http://validator.w3.org/

WebTrends – http://www.webtrends.com

Writing for the Web – http://www.useit.com/papers/webwriting/

Yahoo! – http://www.yahoo.com

Yale C/AIM Web Style Guide – http://info.med.yale.edu/caim/manual/

Index

070.502854678/MIL

070.502854678/MIL